of his career—the translation of *The S[ound]* *and the Fury*. To this day *Le Bruit et la f[ureur]* remains one of the truly superlative Fr[ench] translations of modern American literatu[re.]

Although the focus of the book is on Fa[ulk]ner, it contains essays on the impact of [the] American novel in France and on the American college novel. Also included are selected prefaces to Coindreau's translations of fiction by Erskine Caldwell *(Un Pauvre Type)*, Truman Capote *(Les Domaines hantés)*, William Goyen *(La Maison d'haleine)*, Flannery O'Connor *(La Sagesse dans le sang)*, and William Maxwell *(La Feuille repliée)*.

Long recognized as a critic and translator of distinction, Coindreau's influence on the Continent, and especially in France, can hardly be overestimated. It has been through his perceptive articles and painstaking translations that the French and many other Europeans have come to understand the United States. This book of his essays amounts to a summation of sophisticated French thought towards American fiction in the twentieth century—a period which, from the French point of view, *was* the time of William Faulkner.

GEORGE McMILLAN REEVES received his doctorate in comparative literature from the Sorbonne and is an associate dean of the graduate school at the University of South Carolina. The author of articles in various scholarly periodicals, he has also written *Thomas Wolfe et l'Europe* (Paris, 1955) and edited Flaubert's *Poésies de jeunesse* (Columbia, 1968).

THE TIME OF
WILLIAM FAULKNER

THE TIME OF
WILLIAM FAULKNER

UNIVERSITY OF
SOUTH CAROLINA PRESS

A French View of Modern
American Fiction

Essays By
MAURICE EDGAR COINDREAU
Edited and
Chiefly Translated By
George McMillan Reeves

With a Foreword By
Michel Gresset

COLUMBIA
SOUTH CAROLINA

FIRST EDITION

Published in Columbia, S.C., by the
University of South Carolina Press, 1971

International Standard Book Number: 0-87249-212-5
Library of Congress Catalog Card Number: 74-144804

Manufactured by Kingsport Press, Inc.
Designed by Robert L. Nance

For Carolyn, Geordie, *and* Marianne

CONTENTS

Part Three: CONTEMPORARIES AND SUCCESSORS

Part Four: THE AMERICAN COLLEGE NOVEL

FOREWORD

Whatever the reasons were for the transatlantic migration of
Maurice Edgar Coindreau in 1923 (there is no doubt, however,
that they were poles apart from those of the then active "lost
generation," for Coindreau never counted himself among the
uprooted), perhaps the most striking fact about it is its character of regular, one might even say obstinate, recurrence.
Except for the war period, when he could not leave the
American continent, every single year from 1923 to 1966 saw
him sail or fly back to France during the summertime. Not to
his home town in Vendée, though, but to Paris, where he had
his friends, and where, gradually, he became one of the best-
known and appreciated figures at Gallimard, the publisher of
all his translations.

This double fidelity—to France and to Gallimard—is only the
most outward sign of his attachments. One of his great mottoes
has always been that a translator should "stick to his authors" as
long as he likes them, because only in this way can he become
familiar with the writer's style, which is the necessary condition of excellence. He has always acted upon this idea: he left
Dos Passos for Hemingway, and Hemingway for Faulkner, but he
never left Faulkner for very long. And after Faulkner, he had
much to do with those following the trail that Faulkner had

blazed. Even now, in 1969, at the age of seventy-six, he has just begun work on the third novel by Fred Chappell, whose first book he translated himself and whose second he left to a younger man only because he was then busy with Styron's *The Confessions of Nat Turner.*

As with "his" authors (indeed, some are so much "his" that few realize that Coindreau has translated only six of Faulkner's novels), so with his friends. Few can complain of a breach in Coindreau's loyalty. He seems to have two sets of friends: those of his own generation, many of whom have been leading literary, artistic, or even political figures in France; and those much younger, who came to him out of admiration for the career he had made (without ever bothering to make a career).

Coindreau is a solitary man, who has been able to manage a fair (to him, and to a few others) balance between life and literature, a balance whose secret he alone knows. Sometimes books are used to shy off the drudgery of people; at other times people are welcome to break the drudgery of work. It is easier to penetrate the secret of his translations than that of this inner economy.

He has always believed that (1) one becomes a translator because one cannot be a writer; (2) a good translation is never achieved through a stroke of genius (though this can happen for a word, a phrase, or a title; the test of Coindreau's triumph in this field is his extraordinary gift for translating titles), but after a humble and patient work: "polishing" is one of his favorite words—and activities; (3) a translator must not only steep himself in his original writer's style, mannerisms, and vision of the world, but also in the nearest contemporary equivalent in his own language. It would never occur to him to undertake the translation of William Byrd's *Diaries,* for instance, without first rereading Saint-Simon. Had he tackled Shakespeare, no doubt he would have pilfered the tremendous language crop to be reaped in Rabelais (one of his favorite writers, whose work he lovingly taught at Princeton). If he, instead of Gide, had been passionately interested in Conrad, he would certainly have begun by rereading Pierre Loti, one of the few French sea-writers. He has always held the view that Dilsey, in *The Sound and the Fury*, was not so much a Negro woman as the perennial house servant, the kind he had been extremely familiar with since his childhood in Vendée. He, therefore, had no trouble translating her speech, for unlike less tactful translators of Faulkner, he avoided the pidgin French of the West Indies for the good old speech of all the Dilseys of the world, whatever their color. But had he met with any trouble, he might only have reread Flaubert's "Un Cœur simple."

Coindreau has never translated a single English work (nor has he ever tried his hand at a poem). This is because translation to him is a total activity, cultural rather than strictly literary and involving much more than just technical experience, of which, as one can imagine, he has more than his share. Here again, we find ourselves steering back to his life. His most-traveled road was the Atlantic, not the Channel. Indeed, he discovered London only a few years ago, after he had left America forever.

Translating, for Coindreau, is a cultural activity rooted in experience. He has traveled through most of the United States, and even across the continent in one memorable trip with Julian Green, and yet, his has never been the urban America. His mental landscape is one of solitude (with books and records) in the midst of nature. His retreat to Virginia, at the foot of the beautiful Blue Ridge Mountains, a few dozen miles south of Charlottesville, was not only an act of love, but of logic. There I found him not a jot less familiar with the things of nature than with the innumerable words that Southern writers have (and use!) to describe them. The French specialist of American plants, I once called him, jokingly.

Not scorn, but pity he has for those pent up in urban beehives. He never approved of anything more than of what Mrs.

O'Connor told me when I visited her in Milledgeville, Georgia. After asking me whether I was city- or country-bred, (I had to confess that I lived in Versailles and worked in Paris.) she simply let out, with great kindness, a nonetheless definitive "You miss much" that still rings in my memory.

In the field of literature Coindreau has always been a great ambassador without ever having to be a diplomat. He would come back from New York on an early summer day with a book like *Manhattan Transfer* or a story like "Dry September" already translated in his bag, bring it to Gallimard, and—that was all. No negotiations were necessary. Coindreau's choices have been Coindreau's choices: definitive, self-sufficient, rarely suffering a comment, never (with Gallimard at least) an objection. I doubt whether even now he sees a single error in the long history of his choices (thirty American and thirteen Spanish titles). And this, of course, is because he never translated a book that he would not have liked to have written himself. With him, this is not a manifesto, but at most, a confession. If Coindreau were to write a personal preface to his own work (here is the achievement, indeed, for with him as with all great professional translators, one can speak of an *oeuvre* as of a unique body of deliberate involvements) this would probably be the gist of it.

To us, he is the man who came with Faulkner at a time when everybody was reading Sinclair Lewis. The part he played in the sudden explosion of the American novel in France was a leading one. He prepared the way for Sartre and the Existentialists ten years before Sartre had written *La Nausée* and his articles on Dos Passos and Faulkner. He, not Sartre, "invented" the American novel: to claim this for him is also to plead against the traditional indifference, if not ingratitude, of the literati for the translators. When the vogue of Faulkner flared up, immediately after the Second World War, what had been translated, and by whom? "Dry September" (January 1932); "A Rose for Emily" (Winter 1932); "There Was a Queen"

(August 1933); *Sanctuary* (1933); *As I Lay Dying* (1934); *Light in August* and "That Evening Sun" (1935); *Sartoris* (1937); *The Sound and the Fury* (1938); and *These Thirteen* (1939). Of these, only *Sanctuary, Sartoris,* and part of *These Thirteen* were not signed by Coindreau. Only two books of Dos Passos' had been translated, one of which, *Manhattan Transfer* (1928), signed by Coindreau, was the very first of the whole series we now call the American novel. Five books by Hemingway had been published in France by 1940, two of them, *A Farewell to Arms* and *The Sun Also Rises* (respectively 1932 and 1933) by Coindreau; by Caldwell, three, two of them, *God's Little Acre* (1936) and *Tobacco Road* (1937) by Coindreau; by Steinbeck, only one, *Of Mice and Men* (1939), again by Coindreau.

But the same could be said of younger novelists, born between the two world wars: Truman Capote, William Goyen, Flannery O'Connor, and William Styron, and yet again of the generation that was born while he was translating the "big five": Reynolds Price, Fred Chappell, Heather Ross Miller, all of whom he "discovered" for us and helped with his quiet but deliberate action.

Just as the part he played is great, so is his responsibility. Let one only think that millions of Frenchmen (and even other nationalities, as some translations into other Romance languages were based on his!) have discovered Faulkner by reading not Faulkner, as Faulkner himself remarked when, in 1937, Coindreau set himself to the challenging task of translating *The Sound and the Fury,* but Coindreau. (He did it so well, indeed, that the novel is clearer in French than in the original at times, as it ought to be since the French language has no neuter pronoun.) Few readers have actually realized this, but even fewer know to whom they are indebted.

We owe Coindreau, I might say again, to certain accidental reasons for his transatlantic migration, but this is obviously not the heart of the matter. The deep secret, to me, lies in the seeds sown in a wonderfully steady and ready mind by the French culture of the beginning of this century. Let one remember that at this time Zola was being overthrown by Gide and Proust; Massenet and Saint-Saëns by Debussy and Ravel; Ingres by Manet, Renoir, and Cézanne; Hugo by Baudelaire, Verlaine, and Rimbaud. Even now, Coindreau has remained faithful to the teeming *renouveau* of French Symbolism. He who wrote a preface to the translation of *The Sound and the Fury* explaining this intricate work in musical terms would certainly agree with Walter Pater and with most of the French Symbolists that "all art constantly aspires towards the condition of music." His sense of language as a medium, his appreciation of the boldest metaphor, his understanding of the finest renderings of synaesthesia have their roots in the lessons taught by the French and European masters of the turn of the century. Like them, he has become a master craftsman for whom there is no higher ethic than in one's own demanding aesthetics. As Baudelaire wrote to Swinburne, ". . . every work of art that is *well done,* naturally and necessarily suggests a *moral.*"

He who smiles with his familiar self-debunking irony whenever he is called a pioneer or an ambassador will not, I hope, disapprove of my final quotation from a poem rather debunkingly called "Two Tramps in Mud Time," in which Robert Frost, another master craftsman, has written:

> My object in living is to unite
> My avocation with my vocation.

No one has better succeeded in this task, both privately and publicly, than Maurice Edgar Coindreau.

MICHEL GRESSET

Versailles, July 14, 1969

INTRODUCTION

Translator, critic, chronicler of literary trends, Maurice Edgar
Coindreau for forty-five years has been an interpreter of American culture to his native France. Born in La Roche-sur-Yon
in 1892, he took a law degree at the University of Bordeaux
before going to Madrid to study Spanish and to teach in a *lycée*
there. During his years in Spain immediately following World
War I, he began his literary career by translating several Spanish plays into French. He first came to the United States
in 1923 when he received a one-year appointment as an in-
structor in modern languages at Princeton University. The
appointment was a fortunate one, and Professor Coindreau remained at Princeton until his retirement in 1961. Meanwhile
he translated into French thirty volumes of American and
Spanish fiction, not to mention plays and individually published short stories; he published textbooks and several volumes
of criticism, as well as scores of prefaces, articles, and reviews.
In 1954 his version of William Goyen's *The House of Breath*
won the Halperine Kaminski Prize for the best European
translation of the year. For his good offices as a literary and
cultural intermediary, the French government in 1955 made
him a *Chevalier de la Légion d'Honneur*. In 1966 Maurice

Coindreau returned permanently to France, where he continues to write and translate.

The busiest part of Professor Coindreau's long and stable career coincided with the rise and decline of the "lost generation" and of the vogue of twentieth-century American fiction in France. The first American novel that he offered to the French public was John Dos Passos' *Manhattan Transfer* in 1928. Beginning with that book, he translated two dozen volumes of our most distinguished fiction, much of it by the "big five" whose works were especially appreciated in France. Among the novels Maurice Coindreau selected to translate, Hemingway is represented by *A Farewell to Arms* (1932) and *The Sun Also Rises* (1933); Caldwell by *God's Little Acre* (1936), *Tobacco Road* (1937), *Poor Fool* (1945), and *Tragic Ground* (1948); Steinbeck by *Of Mice and Men* (1939); and Faulkner by *As I Lay Dying* (1934), *Light in August* (1935), *The Sound and the Fury* (1938), *The Wild Palms* (1952), *Requiem for a Nun* (1957), and *The Reivers* (in collaboration with Raymond Girard, 1964). There are also volumes of short stories by Faulkner and Caldwell. A later generation to receive the special care that goes into every Coindreau translation includes William Maxwell, Truman Capote, William Goyen, William Styron, and Flannery O'Connor. The translator's most recent selections have been Dos Passos' *The Best Times* (in collaboration with Claude Richard), William Styron's *The Confessions of Nat Turner,* and Fred Chappell's *Dagon.*

This list of books and authors is in itself a clear indication of Coindreau's remarkable literary judgment. Most of the works were quite recent when he chose them, and some were relatively obscure. It was critical taste, and never the best-seller lists, that served as his guide. Take, for example, Erskine Caldwell's *Poor Fool.* It is still known to very few in the United States, but despite its ungrammatical crudities it is a powerful nightmare about hoods and monsters who are uniquely American. Coindreau made this novel available to thousands of

Frenchmen, who consequently know something about Erskine
Caldwell that most American readers do not know.

For a considerable number of his translations Coindreau has
written his own prefaces, and some of these prefatory essays,
which have remained practically unknown in America, are
among the most evocative commentaries available on the books
they treat. They do not represent a critical system; they are
acts of practical criticism developing, in each case, out of a
knowledge of the text in question that could hardly be exceeded
except by that of the author himself at the time of the original
creation. Written under the pressures of a very busy literary
life, they are not flawless, but they always provide more than
enough insight to compensate for an occasional discrepancy.

The present collection includes nine of these prefaces, along
with ten articles from literary journals and a two-part survey
of the American college novel. Most of Coindreau's survey
articles—such as those on Steinbeck, Caldwell, Faulkner, and
Wolfe (all in *Aperçus de littérature américaine*) —have been
omitted because they contain a good deal of introductory material that is commonplace in the United States.

The most auspicious event in Coindreau's early career was
his discovery of William Faulkner's novels. In 1931 he published the first article in French on Faulkner ("William Faulkner," *La Nouvelle revue française,* June, 1931). In 1932 he
published the first French translations of stories by Faulkner:
"Septembre ardent," *La Nouvelle revue française* (January) ;
and "Une Rose pour Emilie," *Commerce* (Winter) . Meanwhile
he had completed a translation of *As I Lay Dying* and placed
it with Gallimard, who, for editorial reasons, held it until after
they had published R. N. Raimbault's version of the more
sensational *Sanctuary* in 1934.*

Thus began a relationship that lasted for more than thirty
years and gave an additional dimension to the translator's ca-

* *See* Michel Gresset, "Valery Larbaud et les débuts de Faulkner en France,"
Preuves (June 1966) , pp. 26–28.

reer. Between 1931 and 1963 he added more than a dozen articles and prefaces, most of them in French, to his bibliography of Faulkner criticism. Until now these pieces have gone uncollected. The eleven that are presented here in chronological sequence tell the full story of Coindreau as champion and lifelong friend of William Faulkner. They also give an indication of the important role that Coindreau played in the rise of Faulkner's reputation abroad.

Enough time has passed now to permit the assumption that the French have adopted Faulkner permanently, as they did Poe in the nineteenth century. It would be a mistake, however, to put too much stress on the agency of any one person in the Faulkner phenomenon, whether that person be Maurice Edgar Coindreau, R. N. Raimbault, Valery Larbaud, André Malraux, Claude-Edmonde Magny, or Jean-Paul Sartre. Coindreau himself remarks that literary nations take what they need from other nations. But in this instance there was more than need involved. French readers and critics felt that they had affinities with Faulkner in theory, in technique, and in the set of values which he maintained. Perhaps it was not so much that they needed him as it was that they saw themselves in him—as Baudelaire had seen himself in Poe. This—or at least the illusion of it—being the case, probably no one could have prevented Faulkner from entering the mainstream of French literature. But he was fortunate to have a Coindreau to recognize his talent at an early stage and to translate and introduce such complicated novels as *The Sound and the Fury, Light in August,* and *The Wild Palms.*

Living in the United States, Coindreau knew the American idiom better than did most of his rival translators, and he also knew William Faulkner. When confronted with difficult passages in *The Sound and the Fury,* he was able to discuss them with the author and thus to give his translation unusual authority. For *Light in August*—which he correctly translated as *Lumière d'août,* notwithstanding the belief held by many

Americans for a long time that *light* was used as an adjective in the title—he wrote the frequently cited preface that opened the subject of Faulkner's puritanism. His preface to *The Wild Palms* is one of the first essays to recognize the unity of that novel, as well as the rich resonances of its counterpoint. It may be instructive to point out, in passing, that in his survey article on Faulkner (see *Aperçu de littérature américaine*), written before he had translated the two-stranded novel, Coindreau had some doubt about the interrelationship of the two stories "Old Man" and "Wild Palms." But his intimacy with the text in the act of translation revealed many secrets to him.

The final essay on Faulkner shows an impatience with Americans, a querulousness, that seems exaggerated. It is quite true that the general American public did not in 1963 and does not today recognize Faulkner for what he was. Bernard Shaw might have said of Americans what he said of the English—that they did not deserve to have great men of letters, so little did they honor them. Nevertheless, in 1963 there were undoubtedly more Faulkner studies under way in the United States than in all the rest of the world combined. If Coindreau's strictures seem too severe, they should be considered against the background facts that Faulkner was recognized early in France, that he was elevated to the highest rank of contemporary writers there, and that his works in French not only have sold in enormous numbers but have never been out of print.

Always on the lookout for new talent, Coindreau has champoined a number of lesser-known American writers. Especially noteworthy in this regard are the prefaces to William Goyen's *The House of Breath* and William Maxwell's *The Folded Leaf.* The latter novel Coindreau regards as the most sensitive and accurate account of American college life yet written. In *The House of Breath* he finds depths which readers unschooled in the psychoanalytical animism of Gaston Bachelard might never suspect. Incidentally, Bachelard read the translation of Goyen's novel and wrote to Coindreau, "I wish I could have known about this work when I was writing 'La Maison onirique' in a chapter of *La Terre et les rêveries du repos.*"

The preface to Flannery O'Connor's *Wise Blood* differs from the other prefaces in that very little of it directly concerns the book it introduces. A famous American writer originally supplied a preface for the translation but Miss O'Connor rejected it. Consequently, Coindreau wrote the kind of introductory essay which he felt the French public would need, and his practical solution to an awkward problem won Miss O'Connor's approval. Protestant evangelism of the American type does not exist in France. To us *Wise Blood* is filled with the ironies of a very common aspect of American life; to an uninitiated French reader it would undoubtedly appear as a highly imaginative piece of expressionistic exotica, difficult to relate to reality. Coindreau decided to bridge the gap between *homo Americanus* and Continental man by offering his own summary account of American evangelism. He tells us nothing we did not know. His sources are available to everyone. In addition, some readers may be unhappy to find him placing Mary Baker Eddy, Billy Sunday, and Aimee Semple McPherson in the same category. But there are always new perceptions to be gained by changing our vantage point. The preface to *Wise Blood* is presented here in the cause of seeing ourselves as others see us. Flannery O'Connor, from her isolated Catholic viewpoint in Georgia, had achieved this kind of perspective on her own.

The chronicle of the American college novel attempts to examine one type of fiction over a period of forty-four years. Part I comes from *Aperçus de littérature américaine,* Coindreau's survey of American fiction from the twenties to the mid-forties. Part II was written for the forthcoming new edition of that work. The author tells us that there are no good college novels (although he was willing to make an exception after translating *The Folded Leaf*) and proceeds to emphasize his point by reviewing some of the worst novels ever written. Any student of American fiction could add some interesting titles to the list, but very few will have heard of all the ephemeral novels which Coindreau includes. In addition to having its bibliographical uses, especially for the cultural historian, this two-part chronicle provides a diverting overview of several decades of American university culture.

Despite all his years in America, Maurice Edgar Coindreau has maintained a consistently French outlook. His reference points are always the great French authors, from Rabelais to Gide, from Montaigne to Sartre. The extent to which his views represent French literary taste is sharply illustrated by the essay entitled "Thomas Wolfe ou l'apprenti sorcier," first published in *Quadrille Américain, II,* one of two wartime volumes of criticism that were later absorbed into *Aperçus de littérature américaine.* With swift pen strokes Coindreau sketched Wolfe's life and career—his grandiose ambitions, his inadequacies— and declared that he was a "sorcerer's apprentice" who never achieved the control required by the art of the novel. This was written at a time when Wolfe's posthumous books were fresh and critics were praising them extravagantly. No doubt Coindreau's judgment of Wolfe is too severe, but it is entirely consistent with the general and almost undeviating French insistence on formal excellence in all art. And the handful of French critics who have tried to find merit in the Gant-Webber novels have had no success with the reading public, which, despite adequate translations of all his major books, has never shown a significant interest in Wolfe.

Almost all Coindreau's work has been aimed toward a French public; to read him is like overhearing an interpreter explain us and our literature to his compatriots. Much of what he has said should have been overheard in this country long ago. Perhaps the present volume will help to make up for our neglect of the most prestigious translator of American fiction into French.

GEORGE M. REEVES

Columbia, S.C.
January 1, 1971

PART ONE

THE AMERICAN NOVEL
IN FRANCE

FRANCE AND THE

CONTEMPORARY AMERICAN

NOVEL*

In my career as translator I have often been reproached for my choice of works, and many Americans will not pardon me for having made certain writings of Dos Passos, Hemingway, Faulkner, and Erskine Caldwell known in France. "Why," they say, "present to the foreigner the most unpleasant side of our society, why run the risk of giving a false idea of what is happening on the other side of the Atlantic? Nations are only too prone to slander one another without having weapons supplied them by critics and men of letters." And they do not fail to remind me of all the wrong which was done France by those famous yellow-backed novels which at the turn of the century Americans dared read only in secret.

This reproach, inspired by the best of intentions, shows an almost complete ignorance of the intellectual interests of France, as well as of the attitude of the enlightened public to whom the works in question are addressed. The education of this public dates from a distant past. It has its source in the aesthetics of the seventeenth century, which will fashion French taste for a long time to come, if not forever.

* Translated from the unpublished French text by Madeline Ashton, in *The Kansas City University Review*, III, No. 4 (1937), pp. 273–79. Copyright, University of Kansas City, 1937. Reprinted by permission of the editors and the translator.

II

The universality of art is one of the favorite subjects of lecturers. It contains more oratorical possibilities than truth, and I do not hesitate to say that this Utopia is, like any Utopia, extremely dangerous. Art which had become universal would cease *ipso facto* to be an art. With all due apologies to internationalists, art is essentially a national product, and in every work of art there will be some aspects which only the natives will be able fully to appreciate. Races are just as different as individuals, and to wish to apply to them a universal art is as absurd as to claim to make a costume that everyone would be able to wear with equal elegance.

This does not mean that every intellectual contact with the foreigner is impossible. There are fields of understanding of which the boundaries are limited by the peculiar nature of each country or by the needs of the moment. Readers act like those travelers who seek in foreign countries only what resembles their own countries most. La Rochefoucauld said, "We can love nothing except with relation to ourselves, and we are only following our own taste and our own pleasure when we prefer our friends to ourselves." The skillful editor who wishes to place foreign works in his country will then have to be, above everything else, a psychologist and must know exactly the characteristics of his race.

The Frenchman is essentially a realist. He was so in the Middle Ages when he composed his *fabliaux* just as he is today. But strangely it seems that his realism has need from time to time to acquire new strength from foreign sources in order to preserve its integrity. It is thus that, at the end of the nineteenth century, the influence of Ibsen contributed largely to the success of Antoine and Lugné-Poë, as earlier Balzac had need to read Walter Scott in order to construct his *Comédie Humaine*. The same phenomenon is still more evident in the musical domain. When, after the Wagnerian rage, Debussy, advised by Erik Satie, was trying to restore music to a level closer to nature, it

was toward Russia that he turned, toward the works of Moussorgsky, whose *Boris Godounov* is the direct ancestor of *Pélléas
et Mélisande.* In these three cases we see the artists seeking beyond their frontiers: first, the psychological truth which is hidden under the symbols of the great Norwegian; second, realism
at the service of material essentially romantic; and, finally, a
music which avoided mystic exaltation and approached as
nearly as possible human language.

A novel will please in France only if it contains an exact picture of life. Hence certain demands: the Frenchman expects
that the author be a good psychologist, one who is unsatisfied
with superficial observation. The mask which each of us puts
over his face in order to deceive his neighbor and himself interests him only insofar as the novelist succeeds in lifting it. He
likes to know what there is behind the actions of men. Profoundly skeptical, he is of a distrustful nature. Sometimes he
lets himself be dazzled, for he has a mind open to novelties, but
if he perceives that this novelty is of poor alloy, he does not
hesitate to fight it as ardently as he had defended it. Hence, in
the sixteenth century, a poet like Joachim du Bellay, after having Petrarchized according to the fashion, wrote a poem *Contre
les Pétrarquistes;* hence also the attacks of Molière, Boileau,
and La Bruyère against *préciosité,* and the oblivion into which
the theater of Victor Hugo or that of Edmond Rostand has
fallen. On the other hand the tragedies of Racine have lost
nothing of their prestige, any more than such works as *La
Princesse de Clèves, Madame Bovary, A la Recherche du temps
perdu*—works built on a rock with materials of first quality,
knowledge of the human heart with its glories and its weak-
nesses, courageous vision of society *sans fard ou couverture* as
du Bellay said, and little action, since for the cultured Frenchman the intrigue of the novel is not what attracts him. Nor do
the ideas, so far as that is concerned. He knows how ephemeral
their interest is and that a good comedy of character is worth
more than all the thesis plays of Dumas fils and Brieux.

One will understand now why it is toward the most realistic American writers that the editors turn by preference. They find in Sinclair Lewis, Dreiser, Sherwood Anderson, and the representatives of the postwar school a frank and courageous vision of existence, not to mention the documentary value so precious to a people always curious to know what their scorn of traveling prevents them from observing firsthand. That is why to those who reproach me for never having done anything for Miss Willa Cather, I can only answer that I know no serious editor in Paris who would be interested in her books. Perhaps they would have been well received at the end of the last century when even some cultured people read Octave Feuillet and Georges Ohnet, but the present generation is more exacting. It would object to the novels of Willa Cather as being too serious for children and too puerile for grown people, and one can easily understand why the translations of *Shadows on the Rock* passed completely unnoticed. In the presence of that little girl who, at Quebec in the seventeenth century, is astonished that her bedfellows did not wash their feet before going to bed, I am certain that every Frenchman, having reached the age of reason, would call Miss Cather's attention to the fact that at Versailles at the same period King Louis XIV himself did not even wash his hands. She would be advised to read Saint-Simon to inform herself about the customs of the time, and some one would recall to her the famous remark of André Gide: *"C'est avec les beaux sentiments qu'on écrit les mauvais livres."*

The vogue which the new American literature enjoys today comes also from a different cause. It happens periodically that countries feel the need of rejecting the old traditions and of hurling themselves into the unexplored realms of novelties. That is what Spain did around 1898 with writers like Pio Baroja, Azorín, Valle-Inclán, Jacinto Benavente. It is what France did several times but particularly with the postwar flowering of the surrealist movement prepared some years beforehand by Lautréamont and Guillaume Apollinaire. These literary revolutions are always the indication of more or less profound disturbances of *sensibilité*, the manifestation of states of *inquiétude* as Benjamin Crémieux has so justly described it—in short, of malady. Now all the world knows that nothing consoles a sick person so much as to know that he has brothers in misfortune. A psychological truth too often misunderstood is hidden in Peter Arno's "Now tell me all about your operation." Restless France of the postwar period turned to restless America as the young romantics of 1830 turned to Germany, the fatherland of Werther, and to England, the country of Byron. And now that social problems are the order of the day, it is again in America that France finds the greatest number of young writers who are occupied with the same problems.

Finally there is a third element that one must never lose sight of when trying to understand the interest or indifference manifested by France towards foreign works. I mean technique. It is not by chance that La Bruyère said that to make a book is a craft just like making a clock. And the cultured French reader demands of writers that they know their craft. A book constructed without art has very little chance of pleasing; while, on the other hand, a book in which there may be nothing but purely technical qualities may very well receive only eulogistic criticisms. That is another reason why the novels of Miss Cather will never interest the French public. The elegance of style disappearing in translation, there remain only badly constructed stories, without harmony between the elements which compose them, books of a well-endowed beginner.

III

These three points established, it will be easy for us to explain the reaction of French critics to American works recently published in France.

There are at the present time in Paris three important collections devoted to the propagation of foreign works: *Les Feux Croisés* of the publishing house Plon, *Le Cabinet Cosmopolite*

of Stock, and the collection *Du Monde Entier* of Gallimard
(N. R. F.) . The publishing house of Rieder has also published
modern works of value like *One Man's Initiation* by John Dos
Passos (*L'Initiation d'un homme*) and *Expression in America*
by Ludwig Lewisohn under the title *Psychologie de la littérature
américaine.*

N. R. F., as is to be expected, is of all these publishers the
most audacious and enterprising. While others devote them-
selves to the realists of the first period—Sinclair Lewis, Dreiser,
Bromfield—Gallimard insists on remaining in the vanguard of
American production as it has remained in the vanguard of
French production. It was one of the first to publish Sherwood
Anderson (*Winesburg, Ohio*) and Waldo Frank (*City Block*).
Frequently it assures itself of the right of priority to the com-
plete work of an author, reserving the right to give it up
temporarily if the production of the author ceases to please it.
Thus in the work of Dos Passos, Gallimard reserved for itself
Manhattan Transfer and *In All Countries.*

The interest awakened by *Manhattan Transfer* was very
great. The book possessed the three qualities required to attract
the respect of the enlightened French public. For the first time
the French saw New York as they imagined it was, with all the
miseries and turpitudes of large cities. They felt life swarming
in it, and they were interested in the heroes because they saw
in the characters the same restlessness which obsessed them at
the time. They saw Jimmy Herf as similar to the people which
the postwar period had produced in Europe—those *déracinés*
of whom Philippe Soupault traced such a moving portrait in
his novel *A la Dérive.* There was communion of souls; consequently, comprehension and sympathy. Finally, the technique
of the novel was extremely skillful, very *couleur du temps* in
its cinematographic flickering. That was an experiment calculated to awaken the interest of all novelists, and Jules Romains,
who had had a foreshadowing of it in *Mort de quelqu'un,* had

only to give it more ample proportions to construct *Les Hommes de bonne volonté.* Ernest Hemingway had a much more limited success. After a volume of short stories: *Cinquante mille dollars,* N. R. F. published first *L'Adieu aux armes,* then *Le Soleil se lève aussi.* The first volume had a preface by Drieu La Rochelle, the second by Jean Prévost. The latter was able to see what makes for the weakness of the work of Hemingway—the impossibility of the author to escape from himself. "Certainly," he wrote, "Hemingway is not at all a moralist and very little an analyst." That is sufficient to explain why his popularity in France, if he ever had any, was of very short duration. He amused, for, as Drieu La Rochelle wrote, he introduced a little of brutal life; but "a barbarian, restless, subtle, fragile—like all barbarians," his domain was too limited to enjoy eternal life.

The opposite has been the result with regard to William Faulkner, whom French criticism considers today as one of the most interesting authors not only of American literature but of the literature of all countries. Two stories had already appeared, "Septembre ardent" (N. R. F.) and "Une Rose pour Emilie" *(Commerce)*, when Gallimard published *Sanctuaire* with a preface by André Malraux. The translation of *As I Lay Dying* was also ready at that moment, and there was a long discussion on the question of which of these two books should appear first. The danger which *Sanctuaire* might present was exorcised by Malraux's admirable preface. At the very first stroke the author of *La Condition humaine* was able to show the reader that under the excess of the plot was hidden a depth which many American critics, hypnotized by the corncob, had not seen. "As Lawrence is wrapped up in sexuality," he wrote, "Faulkner buries himself in the irremediable. A dull force, at times epic, is unleashed in him as soon as he succeeds in bringing face to face one of his characters and the irremediable, and perhaps the irremediable is his only true subject, perhaps for him the only object is to succeed in crushing man." It is unusual that a critic should succeed in anticipating with such acuteness the future work which lies germinating in an early novel. This phrase of Malraux is in fact a whole analysis of *Light in August* and *Absalom, Absalom!*, where one could also find the epic elements which already existed in the embryonic state in *Sanctuaire*.

It is on this same epic element that Valery Larbaud based the preface which he composed for *Tandis que j'agonise*. An erudite commentator of Joyce's *Ulysses*, Larbaud interprets the novel of Faulkner as a sort of odyssey in which the peasants become princes conducting the deceased queen to the cemetery. The funeral procession of Addie Bundren has in fact the grandeur of the *chansons de geste*, like certain rustic tragedies of Ramón del Valle-Inclán (*Voces de Gesta, Romances de Lobos*, or *Divinas Palabras*). But there is more than that in *As I Lay Dying*; there is a technique which Valery Larbaud compares very justly to a machine for reading or projecting thought, "a sort of reflector which the novelist turns on each of his characters in turn."

I have myself insisted on the importance of this technique in the preface which I have prepared for my translation of *Light in August*, and I have tried also to emphasize the importance of the fundamental puritanism which explains so many aspects of the work of Faulkner. Published under the title (false but poetic) *Lumière d'août*[1], this novel has raised to the heights the reputation of Faulkner in France. "Prodigious book" according to Jean Paulhan. "A terrifying book, full of genius," according to René Trintzius. "The whole story is conducted with an art without reprieve, at times breathless, with an astonishing sense of intimation and of the inexpressible. The pages which precede the murder, in this regard, belong among

---

[1] When Coindreau wrote this article, he apparently had been led to believe that his translation of the title was in error, that *light* was used as an adjective instead of a noun. In 1937 he learned from Faulkner himself that the translation was correct. See "On Translating Faulkner" and "The Faulkner I Knew" in this volume.

the greatest," wrote Pierre Humbourg. "Of the three books already offered to the French public, it is certainly in *Lumière d'août* that one can best grasp, in its amplitude and its power, the art—full, violent, bitter, and diabolical—of this extraordinary visionary," said Pierre Loewel. As for Ramon Fernandez, he estimates that Faulkner has become "the best qualified representative of a fashion of writing which has an original and fertile place in international letters." These few citations show all that American literature owes to this writer who, for many still, is only an emissary of the devil. And it was not necessary to be a sorcerer to guess that the success of Faulkner was assured in France. A psychological acuteness which digs down into the most concealed folds of the subconscious, a technique entirely new although based on elements already known (stream of consciousness, for example). Nothing else was necessary to conquer the esteem of the French intellectuals.

God's Little Acre (under the title *Le Petit Arpent du bon Dieu*) has appeared too recently for me to be able to judge the attitude of the critics with regard to it. Prefaced by André Maurois, this audacious novel has already, however, shocked the conservative press which recommends respectable families to keep it out of their libraries. But it is probable that the enlightened public will welcome it. There is already talk of a theatrical adaptation. In any case if it is probable that the critics will recognize the inferiority of the art of Caldwell to that of Faulkner; at least they will not deny the documentary interest offered by works like *Le Petit Arpent du bon Dieu* and *La Route au tabac,* which has been published with an introduction by Marcel Aymé.

For the same reason, the works of J. T. Farrell are in process of translation, and already the French have been able to read the first volume of the trilogy of *Studs Lonigan.* If the technique of this work is questionable, if one may reproach Farrell with violating too often the precept of Boileau: *"Qui ne sait se borner ne sut jamais écrire,"* one must recognize in him the art of creating characters and of describing a world which except for him would be practically inaccessible to us.

Finally it is not rare to see novels of secondary importance translated into French. Recently James M. Cain's *Le Facteur sonne toujours deux fois* appeared with a preface by Irene Nemirovsky. The works of Dashiell Hammett have also been published. That is because there is in them a kind of literature very original for France, which is less at ease with the brutal style than with the novel of analysis. Moreover, the Frenchman finds again in these stories of murder and of orgies an aspect of America with which the cinema has already made him familiar, and which entertains him by the contrast which it offers with the manners of his own country, less muscular and less intense.

IV

Let the Americans concerned about the reputation of their country cease then to be worried. Far from harming its glory, the books which are appearing today in Paris only contribute to assure America the place it deserves in the world of letters. They should know that if the novels translated presented an idyllic America, cities in which all the Christian virtues flourished, the French would not read them, for they would know that they are false. They are too old to have any illusions about human nature. They know that in all latitudes men are always the same. They would not be deceived by hypocritical novelists. There is no danger of seeing them generalize. They are too accustomed to reading to fall into that childish vice. Because they have liked the works of Faulkner, they will not believe that lynching Negroes is the daily occupation of Americans, any more than they will believe that ladies in the United States have a habit of conserving, like Miss Emily, corpses in a state of decomposition in their bedrooms. One must not forget that, until recently, American literature was as a whole only a very weak offspring of English literature. And the little reputation that it had, it owed to writers like Edgar Poe and Walt Whitman who caused many of their compatriots to frown. The ways of God are impenetrable, and the Holy Scripture tells us that often the most beautiful actions are performed by the greatest sinners. It is a *poète maudit,* Arthur Rimbaud, to whom Paul Claudel owed his conversion to Catholicism. It is to the writers who paint it under the blackest colors that America owes today the worldwide reputation of its literature. Is there anyone ungrateful enough to reproach them for it?

FROM BILL CODY

TO BILL FAULKNER*

For a quarter of a century I have heard some Americans express a deep concern about the harm that the American novels exported to Europe might do to the reputation of the United States. "Aren't you afraid," say these well-meaning friends, "that these objectionable tales of alcoholic orgies, murders, rapes, and lynchings, so often expressed in terms equally objectionable, will give a wrong and most regrettable picture of our way of life?" My answer is invariably negative and is followed by a question, "Does the reputation of England suffer from the accumulation of horrors which one finds in Shakespeare's plays, and does God's reputation suffer from the accumulation of horrors one finds in the Holy Bible?" The pious old lady who reads Absalom's story in the Book of Samuel without any qualms has no right to object if a translator puts Faulkner's version of the same story on the European market.

I presume that when Baudelaire translated Edgar Allan Poe and presented him to the French as the greatest poet of his time, many were the Americans who were inclined to resent it. They did not foresee that a few years later the most refined

* Originally published in *The Princeton University Library Chronicle*, XVII, No. 4 (Summer 1956), pp. 185–90. © Princeton University Library, 1956. Reprinted by permission.

school of French poets would base its aesthetics on the poetic principles of this American poet who found his inspiration, as Mallarmé expressed it, *"Dans le flot sans honneur de quelque noir mélange."* Likewise, those who nowadays hold against the translator the exportation of American novels which do not try to prove that life in the United States is heaven on earth do not realize that these novels have not only opened new roads in the field of fiction in general but have made of American literature a reality. They have given it an existence of its own and placed the country which they are accused of slandering in the foreground of the literary scene. Not so long ago, in French universities, American literature was only a part of English literature in general. Of course, the Anglicists studied the great American figures of the nineteenth century, but they were part of their English studies, and no one would have thought of writing on the jacket of a translation of an American book, as is done now, *"Traduit de l'Américain."* The average Frenchman had little or no contact at all with Emerson, Thoreau, or Hawthorne. These authors did not fit into the picture of America which he had built for himself.

This picture was somewhat simple. The United States was a country of Indians and multimillionaires. And this picture, although fragmentary, was nonetheless true. It was formed of elements undeniably real, since they came in a straight line from America itself and were confirmed in big headlines by the press and in satirical novels by French writers of the time.

At the end of the nineteenth century several sensational marriages took place between titled Frenchmen and wealthy American girls who, forgetting for a moment some of their democratic principles, were only too willing to exchange some of dad's millions for a flattering title of nobility and an impressive coat of arms. The French nobility was poor and the temptation was too great to be resisted. In order to prevent touchy ancestors from turning over in their graves, it was not too hard to get them to believe that a bride entering a dilapidated castle with enough money to have it restored to its pre-revolutionary splendor undoubtedly deserved to be called Madame la Duchesse. Unfortunately, dollars and blue blood rarely mixed well, and these marriages as a rule did not turn out very successfully. Clashes between two forms of civilization so different from each other had to be expected. Whenever they happened, the newspapers featured them on their front pages and the satirists in novels which often were best sellers: Abel Hermant's *Les Transatlantiques* (1897), for example. Always cruelly simple, these novels were usually very fair. If the bride with her delusions of grandeur was shown under a not too flattering light, her aristocratic husband and his family did not fare much better. But of these international marriages, no matter how ephemeral, one thing remained: the idea in the mind of the average Frenchman that America was the land of fabulous fortune and New York a city which had only one street, Fifth Avenue, with its impressive mansions.

It was also for us the land of the redskins. I always notice an amused smile on the faces of my American friends whenever I mention that one of the greatest events of the year 1905 in France was the coming of Buffalo Bill with his Wild West Show. Colonel Cody swept us off our feet not because we were surprised by the unusual spectacle, but because this spectacle was exactly what we expected from an American entertainer. The French have always been great readers. They start living with books from the time they know their alphabet. In 1905 I was thirteen years old, and, as a relaxation from the compulsory classwork, I had read not only innumerable fairy tales but nearly everything Jules Verne had written, and the best-known volumes of Fenimore Cooper, which my grandfather kept in his library. I can still remember reading *The Last of the Mohicans* in the attic of my grandparents' country house, with the rain beating on the roof. For hours I lived in the midst of war cries and pistol shots; old trunks became mail coaches, and in the dark corners of the vast storeroom silent canoes would lurk, and lights would appear in a log cabin. Buffalo Bill's Show came as an irrefutable proof that this dream world was a reality. He brought us the American we knew and loved. And by "we" I do not mean only we children but our parents as well, for practically everybody in France was familiar with Cooper's works. This even applied to the few French people who had been in the United States and could have come back with a less romantic, less partial point of view. For them, also, Buffalo Bill was a true symbol of American life. I have found a confirmation of this fact in a letter of Henry de Montherlant, my contemporary, whose grandmother, the Countess de Riancey, née de Courcy, had lived from 1850 to 1870 in New York, where her father represented the Saint-Gobain glass works and defended the cause of Catholicism by means of articles and books, one of which, *The Catholic Church in the United States,* appeared in an English translation in 1856. "My childhood," writes Montherlant, "was lived among American souvenirs brought back from the United States by my great-grandfather: a Florida snake in a glass jar, Indian relics, etc. I learned English with my family and I spoke it with such a pronounced Yankee accent that my English teachers at school objected to it. . . . I remember how enthralled I was when—I was at the time seven or nine years old—Buffalo Bill came to Paris with his show. My grandmother had a long and friendly talk with him and later with the Indians of his company, with whom she even took a few puffs from the celebrated peace pipe. Then the pipe was offered to me, but I refused it bravely. I say bravely because it took more courage on my part to be laughed at for my abstention than to risk a few minutes of nausea." If one remembers that the same grandmother was the grandniece of Claire de Kersaint, Duchess of Duras, a famous friend of Chateaubriand, whose father, Admiral Count de Kersaint, had taken part in the War of Independence on the side of the Americans and, going up the Surinam River, had taken from the British the settlements of Demerara, Essequebo, and Berbice, one will realize

that Buffalo Bill was a great American figure as much for the
highest and most cultured society as for the young readers of
Fenimore Cooper, Mayne Reid, and their French imitators.

After the First World War the picture changed radically.
Wealthy heiresses and Indians in full regalia had been replaced
by thousands of doughboys, less likely to create in the minds of
the French romantic visions in exotic settings. The American
soldier, although wearing a uniform much cleaner and better
fitted than that of the French *poilu*, was a soldier just the same.
We used to see them playing baseball on the sidewalks, buying
candy for children, and flirting with nursemaids in the parks.
One would have thought that life was as simple for them as for
the children of whom they seemed so fond. This was so much
the more puzzling since in France at that time the young
generation was entering a phase of great spiritual restlessness
combined with a feverish desire to reconstruct the world on
such foundations that another war would be impossible. Could
these apparently carefree American young men have problems
of that sort? After leaving French soil, what would their life
be, to what cities would they go, what were those cities like?
Cooper could no longer give us the answers. Neither could
Edith Wharton. Her public, the conservative readers of the
Revue des Deux Mondes, had begun to realize that her universe
was very limited and more apt to throw a light on the behavior
of the wealthy heiresses than on the friendly soldiers who late
at night could be seen dead drunk on the very same benches
in the parks where they had spent their more innocent
afternoon.   ʄ

Life in the big city: for years already several French writers,
sociologists, philosophers, novelists, and poets had been fasci-
nated by its complexity. Zola had tried to bring out the souls of
three towns: Lourdes, Rome, and Paris. Following in the foot-
steps of Emile Verhaeren, poet of *Les Villes Tentaculaires*
(1896), Jules Romains, in 1908, had published *La Vie
Unanime. Men of Good Will* was already in the depths of his

subconscious. The ground was prepared to receive any seed that would develop into a novel of a big city. Dos Passos' *Manhattan Transfer* came out in France in 1928. I consider this date as the point of departure of what Mme Claude-Edmonde Magny, in a remarkable volume of essays on American literature, calls *"l'âge du roman américain."* The French found in *Manhattan Transfer* not only what their legitimate curiosity was seeking but also a story presented with an entirely new technique—the only technique which could make possible the portrait of a metropolis within the limits of a single volume. Many were the French writers who could have signed the declaration made by Sinclair Lewis: "In *Manhattan Transfer,* Mr. Dos Passos does, really does, what all of us have frequently proved could not be done: he has given the panorama, the sense, the smell, the sound, the soul, of New York." We knew now that New York was not different from any European metropolis, and we immediately felt closer to the American people. The millionaires and the Indians had become museum pieces. If we did not speak yet of "One World," we could speak of one humanity, equal in ugliness, in suffering, and, occasionally, in joys, no matter on which continent. After 1928 there was not one year that did not see the publication of an important American novel, often presented to the public by well-known French writers: 1932, *A Farewell to Arms,* prefaced by Drieu La Rochelle; 1933, *The Sun Also Rises,* prefaced by Jean Prévost; 1934, *Sanctuary* and *As I Lay Dying,* prefaced by André Malraux and Valery Larbaud respectively; 1935, *Light in August;* 1936, *God's Little Acre,* prefaced by André Maurois; 1937, *Tobacco Road;* 1938, *The Sound and the Fury;* 1939, *Of Mice and Men,* prefaced by Joseph Kessel; etc.

The reasons for the popularity and impact of a foreign literary genre in a particular country at a particular time are always the same. The foreign works act as a kind of blood transfusion. Either they reinforce already existing tendencies, or they bring new elements to genres beginning to show signs of pernicious anemia. Several treatments already had been proposed in France to free the novel from its overemphasis on psychological analysis and on intellectualization in subject matter as well as in form. *Unanimisme, cosmopolitisme, populisme,* and general glorification of violent physical action (sports, revolution) were manifestations of a reaction against a literature too strictly confined within the four walls of the writer's study. Dos Passos, Hemingway, Caldwell, Steinbeck, and Faulkner brought the French what they needed. They did it with power, originality, and skill, and they did it in a credible way. That is to say, without trying to hide certain facts in order to make their readers believe that life in America is different from life in European countries. In the United States, as everywhere else, vice and virtue, wealth and poverty, live side by side, and it would be very easy to prove that in the majority of American novels which are accused of presenting the worst aspects of American life the number of admirable characters is about equal to the number of villains. How many times have I heard that *The Sound and the Fury* (to mention only this novel) is a horrible picture of idiocy, sadism, immorality, and what not? But the censors forgot that the most important character in the book is Dilsey, undoubtedly one of the most exemplary figures of a woman ever to appear in fiction. Why should we hold against Faulkner one Temple Drake, the disreputable heroine of *Sanctuary,* when, on the other hand, he gives us a galaxy of noble and dignified old Southern ladies so dear to his heart that he recreates them in practically every novel under different names?

A few months ago, a man of good will, but of poor psychological insight, suggested that the American government should permit only the exportation of books showing exclusively the best aspects of American life. I do not hesitate to say that the result of such a measure would be disastrous as propaganda. Any European who has come in contact with doughboys, GI's, or American tourists would laugh at such books. They would accuse their authors either of being hypocrites who hide part of the truth in the interests of an obvious propaganda or of being overgrown children unable to see and to express what goes on around them.

Far from ruining his country's reputation, the accused contemporary American novelist has shown to European writers that he is on a par with them, that he can write novels as original, as frank, and as fearless as those produced by the European writers themselves. If Russia, France, and Germany may take pride in a Dostoevsky, a Balzac, and a Thomas Mann, why should not the United States be proud of a Dos Passos or a Hemingway? It is true that only good books should be exported, but by *good* I do not mean books filled with *good* men, marrying *good* girls, living *good,* happy lives with *good,* intelligent children until they die a *good,* exemplary death. I mean good in the artistic sense, books which possess all the qualities that an enlightened public has the right to expect.

This year (1956) President Eisenhower wrote a long letter to novelist William Faulkner, requesting his collaboration in a new program designed to improve cultural contacts and mutual understanding between the United States and the other countries of the world. A far cry from the days when William F. Cody was, in European countries, a symbol of American culture!

PART TWO

WILLIAM FAULKNER

WILLIAM FAULKNER*

In 1929 he was still unknown. A long poem, *The Marble Faun* (1924), and two novels, *Soldier's Pay* (1926) and *Mosquitoes* (1927), had brought him neither fame nor gain. Only a few friends, among them Sherwood Anderson, had been able to see anything more than promise in his early works.

In 1929 *The Sound and the Fury* was a revelation. Soon, with snobbery playing its part, everyone at literary gatherings talked only of this strange book in which horror was mingled with obscenity. In 1930 *As I Lay Dying* aroused a more genuine kind of interest. The snobs were already seeking new enthusiasms. On the other hand, the serious admirers of William Faulkner, those whom *The Sound and the Fury* had interested because of its good qualities rather than its defects, were conscious that the United States had been enriched by the appearance of a powerfully original novelist with extraordinary vitality. The recent publication of *Sanctuary* allows no more doubt. William Faulkner is actually one of the most interesting figures in the young literature of America. *The Sound and the Fury*, an excruciating story of a cursed family, was a deformed,

* From *La Nouvelle revue française*, CCXXXVI (June 1931), pp. 926–30. Reprinted by permission of Gallimard. Translation by G.M.R.

monstrous production, an accumulation of a very rich raw material which lacked only the work of a skilled and rigorous hand. This kind of work William Faulkner has accomplished in *As I Lay Dying* (1930) and *Sanctuary* (1931).

Addie Bundren has demanded that after her death her body be transported to Jefferson, the town of her birth. The coffin is loaded on a wagon and the whole family, Anse, the father, and the children, Cash, Darl, Vardaman, Jewel, and Dewey Dell accompany the body. A storm has washed away the bridges, and it is impossible to use the fords. A long detour is necessary. Nine days go by. The cadaver is decomposing. Vultures hover over the funeral carriage. Some incidents add complications to the difficulties of the road. The wagon turns over in a ford, and in attempting to right it Cash breaks his leg. He concludes the trip lying on his mother's coffin. His brothers have improvised a plaster cast for him, but gangrene developes quickly in the limb, which is too tightly compressed. One night Darl starts a fire that burns down the barn sheltering the wagon. Saved by Jewel, the coffin finally reaches Jefferson, where it is buried according to the wishes of the deceased.

Such is the subject of *As I Lay Dying*. One must not look for an exact chronology in that macabre odyssey. The fifteen characters whose interior monologues are divided into fifty-nine sections sometimes forget to light their lanterns. Nevertheless, there is no serious obscurity. The game of patience to which the author invited his reader has nothing in common with a Chinese puzzle. The well-cut pieces fit together easily and the design appears without effort in all its morbidity. It is only in *Sanctuary*, however, that one really has the impression of an impeccable mechanism in which all the wheels mesh with the precision of clockwork. The central theme is horrible. In a dilapidated house deep in the woods, a degenerate named Popeye violates a girl, Temple, and kills a weak-minded man, Tommy. Goodwin, a bootlegger who owns the house, is accused of the murder. To no avail Horace, the lawyer, attempts to defend him. Goodwin, suspected by the end of the trial of having committed the rape also, is lynched by the crowd, who sprinkle him with gasoline and set him on fire.

All this is quite banal, one might say, and the devotees of the Grand-Guignol have seen much of the same kind of thing. It is certain that, reduced to its plot alone, *Sanctuary* is no more than a crime novel spiced with perverted eroticism. But in the works of William Faulkner the subject is only a pretext for the display of a technique which, in this instance, approaches perfection. To be fair to Faulkner one must forget his themes and consider only the way he deals with them. Then he ceases to be the satanic creator of nightmares and becomes the virtuoso, the master of a new technique based on the power of the unexpressed.

"That was when I learned that words are no good; that words dont ever fit even what they are trying to say at," Addie thinks in *As I Lay Dying*.[1] By virtue of this principle, every time that William Faulkner wishes to achieve a powerful effect he replaces words with images and facts with symbols. He no longer narrates, he suggests. The enticing scenes vanish into unfinished sentences which, while keeping one's curiosity aroused, inspire at once the desire and the fear of knowing. Because of the mystery that results from this enigmatic writing, the tragic scenes escape from the banality of melodrama and acquire the hallucinating quality which makes a book by Faulkner difficult to forget.

One cannot separate the Faulknerian technique from the characters which provide its reason for existing. In fact there is absolute accord between the characters and the manner in which they are presented. Faulkner deals only with exceptional individuals, and in this respect his work will never have a documentary value equal to that of the books, say, of Sinclair Lewis. The world he creates is his own world, full of strange-

[1] Quoted from the corrected edition (New York: Random House, 1957), p. 163. All references to *As I Lay Dying* are to this edition.

ness and baseness. He has built it on precise data (sometimes autobiographical) but the historian of the American spirit would not be able to derive much benefit from it. On the other hand the psychiatrist will find in it ample matter for study. Degenerates, madmen, and idiots are William Faulkner's favorite characters. Using his technique of the unexpressed, he makes them into figures of astonishing power. Thus, as Mr. James Burnham has very accurately said, it is through what they cannot say that his heroes achieve greatness.[2] The reader cannot escape the fascination of these unfortunates condemned to silence: Donald Mahon (*Soldier's Pay*), the blind aviator who has lost the power of speech as a result of his injuries; Young Bayard (*Sartoris*), who can do nothing but repeat vague allusions to the death of his twin brother; the taciturn Jewel (*As I Lay Dying*); the innocent Tommy and Popeye, the victim and his murderer (*Sanctuary*); and especially the idiot Benjy, whose inarticulate cries fill *The Sound and the Fury*. The character of these wretched beings is often indicated by a simple detail. This detail often then assumes the value of a symbol. All of Mahon is in the scar which disfigures him. The strange eyes that look "like rubber knobs, like they'd give to the touch and then recover with the whorled smudge of the thumb on them" symbolize all the malignant power of Popeye just as Mélisande's golden hair symbolizes all her beauty. (William Faulkner perhaps owes more to the Symbolists than to James Joyce.)

Beside these main figures in Faulkner's novels we find an abundance of picturesque characters. In this regard *Sartoris* is the most interesting volume. In it we see the clashing of the members of an old Southern family that has fallen into decadence: the grandfather, Bayard Sartoris, called "the Colonel"; his sister, the indomitable Miss Jenny, who is found again, old and unsubdued, in *Sanctuary;* and around these haughty

---

[2] "Trying to Say," *The Symposium: A Critical Review,* II (January 1931), pp. 51–59.

masters, their servants, the devoted Negroes—Simon, the coach-man, the good and faithful dog who, like the admirable Dilsey (*The Sound and the Fury*), bears the weight of the cursed family; and Caspey and Isom, childish, lazy, boastful—all speaking their jargon, laying bare their superstitious souls, sometimes giving lessons in good sense to the unreasonable "white folks." The author evokes all these people in settings that are familiar to him: the Southern states of Tennessee and Mississippi. He never strays from them. He knows every aspect of them, every sound, every play of light, and he evokes their ardent spirits through the magic of a style that quivers with sensuality.

He is sometimes reproached for the morbidity he seems to delight in. *"Le sexe et la mort, porte d'entrée et porte de sortie du monde,"* he wrote in *Soldier's Pay*.[3] These two themes serve as a backdrop for all his novels. In his painting he uses some very raw colors, but he does it much less out of perversity than out of puritanism. Death for him is a synonym for putre-faction, as for a monk in the Middle Ages. He does not try to hide the fate which awaits our human carcass. Villon did not use rosy tones to soften the colors of the hanged. As for love, he views it too from the standpoint of a moralist—I will add, of a severe moralist. The sexual act in the work of William Faulkner is always described as a bestial operation, repulsive or perverse; if the rape of Temple is consummated with the aid of a corncob, the reason is more to debase, to insult the act of the flesh than to show the vile depravity of Popeye. The origin of this attitude is to be found in an old background of imperishable idealism. A passage from *Soldier's Pay* is very significant in this regard. "Do you know," Jones says, "how falcons make love? They embrace at an enormous height and fall locked, beak to beak, plunging: an unbearable ecstasy. While

---

[3] "Sex and death: the front door and the back door of the world. How indissolubly are they associated in us!" *Soldier's Pay*, (New York: Boni & Liveright, 1926), p. 295.

we have got to assume all sorts of ludicrous postures, knowing our own sweat. The falcon breaks his clasp and swoops away swift and proud and lonely, while a man must rise and take his hat and walk out."[4] If Faulkner's heroes could make love in the open sky as falcons do, they would not have such a grudge against women for their alluring coquetries. They suffer because they are not pure spirits and take revenge on reality by making it darker than it is. Incapable of acting like angels, they act like beasts. Like every good American, William Faulkner has his bad seed of idealism and, in his secret garden, indulges in the cultivation of the blue flower.

Every day in his own country he gains new followers. Since Europe has contributed much to his formation, she has little right to ignore him. Perhaps certain readers will prove to be recalcitrant at first. In effect Faulkner treats his public in the manner of those malicious nurses who tease the lips of their babies with their nipples in order to induce them to suck. Many like that teasing, which arouses their gourmandism. Others, not knowing the pleasure of desire, become irritated and howl with impatience. There are some positive minds who will not forgive Faulkner for imposing upon their curiosity by withholding the key to his enigmas until the last pages. The author of *Sanctuary* would not know how to write for those "unhappy few," for he invites to his hide-and-seek parties only those whose intelligence takes pleasure in the subtle rules of the game.

[4] *Ibid.*, p. 227.

PREFACE TO

*LIGHT IN AUGUST**

"*Light in August* (1932) features the castration of its hero, a mulatto named Joe Christmas, who, by way of concluding an ugly affair with a middle-aged white woman, murders her." With this concise, bewilderingly facile pronouncement, a recent book on the American novel[1] sums up the most vigorous, the most profound, and the richest of William Faulkner's novels.

I do not say the most original, much less the most sensational. In 1932 *Light in August* was not a subject of controversy as *The Sound and the Fury* had been in 1929. Nor were there cries of scandal as there had been in 1930 when *Sanctuary* disturbed the censors. There were even some overzealous admirers of Mr. Faulkner who complained that this time their idol had neither astounded nor shocked them. They have since made amends, and most of them have recognized that the less spectacular success of *Light in August* was undoubtedly of a superior kind. Above all they have recognized in this savage and passionate fresco the upshot of the works that preceded it, a summation in which the author, in full possession of the techniques he had

---

* From *Lumière d'août* (Paris: Gallimard, 1935) © Editions Gallimard 1938. Translation by G.M.R.

[1] Harry Hartwick, *The Foreground of American Fiction* (New York: American Book Company, 1934), p. 162.

heretofore employed, was able to amalgamate those techniques in dealing with subject matter almost infinitely rich in possibilities.

Hence it would be a serious error to read *Light in August* as an introduction to Faulkner's art. We should not put the cart before the horse. But this is the indispensable book for all those who, disconcerted upon reading *Sanctuary* and *As I Lay Dying*, wish nevertheless to get to the bottom of these mysterious works in which the most atrocious scenes are veiled by treacherous obscurities. For William Faulkner, no matter what some have said about him, does not use horror gratuitously. His work has a quality of inevitability; and it is not with steady nerves that one should approach it but with an intellect prepared to exert itself, and with all the sympathetic curiosity that this first-rate artist deserves.

William Faulkner is neither a monster nor a madman—even less a writer of pornography. He is a man who was born in the land of puritanism and who, like Robinson Jeffers, continues the line of such writers as Edgar Allan Poe and Ambrose Bierce. Deep in the irremediable, as M. André Malraux has so accurately written,[2] he possesses to the highest degree that "tragic sense of life" that Unamuno analyzed. Fatality envelopes a world in which he sees only horrors, in which men and women, the blind marionettes of Destiny, chessmen in the hands of the supreme Player, know only blood, sensual pleasure, and death. And William Faulkner owes this vision to the puritanism bequeathed him by his ancestors, perhaps by the great-grandfather who wrote *The White Rose of Memphis*, an uplifting novel.[3] I already hear cries of paradox, and no doubt I would not have dared to make an assertion so contrary to established opinion if Mr. Faulkner, in a letter that he himself

[2] Preface to *Sanctuaire*, trans. R. N. Raimbault and Henri Delgove (Paris: Gallimard, 1933), p. iii.

[3] One can see how much interest this hypothesis adds to the figure of the Reverend Gail Hightower, who is incapable of escaping from the influence of his grandfather, killed amid the clash of arms. M.E.C.

wrote to me in 1932, had not acknowledged that he had a "strain of puritanism," but "in its proper sense," he added.[4] By that he meant he was not one of those with tight lips and contorted faces but one of those who find out evil straightaway and cause blood to flow, in the manner of the great inquisitors. Puritanism. Wellspring of fanaticism and, consequently, the best school for hatred, that hatred which is always latent in the works of William Faulkner and which overflows from every page of *Light in August.* How artfully he describes them, these puritans—whether it be McEachern, the obtuse brute, or Doc Hines, the mad mystic, both belonging to the species that provided the United States with John Brown and his confederates, whose bloody prowess *ad majorem Dei gloriam* has been novelized by Leonard Ehrlich in *God's Angry Man.*[5] Their God is a god of anger, vengeance, and hatred, passions which are linked, in the case of Doc Hines, with a phobia of eroticism. But William Faulkner himself has shown definite signs of this phobia ever since he began to write novels. It inspires his most daring pages, in his desire to stigmatize what old Doc Hines likewise regards as "bitchery and abomination." We must regard this old fanatic, then, as more than an episodic character necessary for the development of the plot. In him Faulkner has materialized his own ancestral puritanism, thus furnishing us the key to that aspect of his art for which he has been most often reproached: I mean the debasement of woman and the morbid bestiality of the erotic scenes. In his work we will not find the kind of glorification of fleshly pleasure which, for example, stands out in Erskine Caldwell's *God's Little Acre.* Even less will we see him, as we have seen D. H. Lawrence in *Lady Chatterley's Lover,* weave garlands of forget-me-nots for

[4] Wyndham Lewis, in an article dealing very severely with William Faulkner, calls him "a Calvinist moralist" and "a moralist with a corncob" (*Men Without Art*, pp. 42–64) . M.E.C.

[5] One must go back to the time of the religious wars in the sixteenth century in order to find a French equivalent for this famous American agitator. M.E.C.

John Thomas and Lady Jane. When he speaks of women, it is in the manner of the church fathers. A modern Paphnuce, he regards the daughters of Eve only as so many Thaïses promenading, under the cover of their makeup, the vilest lubricity: Lena Grove and Milly, in such a hurry to be seduced; Miss Atkins, the doctor's Jezebel; Bobbie, the prostitute; and Miss Burden, the nymphomaniac. In addition to lasciviousness, William Faulkner attributes to women an instinct for "cunning and indirection" and "infallibility for the spontaneous comprehension of evil";[6] and he protests, "But what woman, good or bad, has ever suffered from any brute as men have suffered from good women?"[7] For they always win, and the surrender of man takes place, as one could guess, under the most disheartening conditions. Could it be otherwise with a being who is as defective physically as mentally, *"l'enfant malade et douze fois impur"* about whom Vigny complained long ago? In *Light in August* the sexual act is equated to vomiting. And Faulkner prepares the demonstration of this idea with an astonishing psychological sureness by letting Joe Christmas as a child swallow too much toothpaste so that his nausea concides with his discovery of the act of love. For that matter, William Faulkner, who believes in Fate, never leaves anything to chance. He justifies the least gestures of his heroes; and this trait stems, as André Malraux understood so clearly, from the fact that he must "frequently conceive his scenes before imagining his characters . . . and that [his] imagination serves only to bring characters logically to a preconceived situation."[8]

Love seen in such a bad light inevitably kindles hatred in the hearts of those who succumb to it: Christmas strikes the Negress as soon as he feels attracted to her, and the first time he possesses Miss Burden his hands are "hard and urgent," but "with rage

---

[6] *Light in August* (New York: Harrison Smith & Robert Haas, 1932), pp. 117, 245, 250.

[7] *Ibid.*, p. 299. It is Hightower, not the author, who poses this question.

[8] Malraux, *loc. cit.*

alone." Later, when he beats her, he speaks "the words which she had once loved to hear on his tongue . . . murmurous, obscene, caressing."[9] And this hatred (which even when he was a child caused him to cut off the buttons that a loving hand had sewn on and to dump onto the floor the meal that his foster mother had prepared for him), this hatred grows to the extent that the female element in general becomes the object of his horror. If Joe Christmas seeks refuge in the stables, it is because horses "are not women. Even a mare horse is a kind of man."[10] In like manner the monks of Mount Athos close their door to everything that partakes of the feminine sex.

This flight to the stables is only one of the incidents which indicate the frightful moral crisis that the hero undergoes before the crime. In this analysis of the genesis of a murder, William Faulkner matches the greatest writers, not excepting Dostoevsky. To begin with, there is the initial fact: Miss Burden's age, which transforms her from a Messalina into a Saint Theresa, into a living symbol of Joe Christmas's two phobias, the periodical affliction of women (which he had learned about when quite young) and the spirit of charity, of beneficence toward others. The seed of murder, having fallen into the soul of the half-breed, develops slowly, step by step: the arrival of Brown, drunk; the razor under the pillow; and the sudden thought "This is not the right one." Then come the chorus of voices and the insidious phrase "because she started praying over me" followed by the desire for purification (an essentially puritan element) through intimate contact with redeeming nature—a naked excursion through the cool weeds in the hot night. Here William Faulkner joins Sherwood Anderson, who often gave his heroes a desire for lustral nudity.[11] But the image of Miss Burden returns and Christmas is again in the grip of his demon.

---

[9] *Light in August,* pp. 223, 262.
[10] *Ibid.,* p. 101.
[11] Sherwood Anderson wrote a whole book, *Many Marriages,* around this theme. M.E.C.

His walk through the Negro section supplies the final impetus toward madness. And the voice, now an obsession, that says, "She ought not to started praying over me," leads him back to the estate and to that room where the murder is henceforth inevitable. Never before has Mr. Faulkner given us such an acute psychological analysis in such a resplendent style.

Morbid eroticism and excessive cruelty are not the only charges that have been leveled at William Faulkner. Some have complained of his obscurity. In that same book which rates *Light in August* as a simple story of castration, one can read that Faulkner sometimes "becomes more incoherent than Joyce, whose presence is often felt in his pages."[12] But in fact if there is one fault which Mr. Faulkner does not have, it is surely incoherence. His writing techniques are no more arbitrary than his psychology. All they require is to be analyzed and understood. And in this regard, *Light in August,* better than any other novel by Faulkner, will permit the reader who has been stymied by illusory difficulties to disassemble the machinery of a technique that seems rather complex but is in reality quite simple.

Taking up his subject without delay, the author shows us the initial event which will serve as a pivot in the novel: a house burns and the woman who owned it is found with her throat cut. A half-caste who lived on the estate has disappeared. After one of his comrades informs on him, the police set out on his trail. Such is the first act of the tragedy. Act two: the motives of the crime. Through a series of scene-shifts Faulkner returns to the criminal's past and undertakes a genuine *recherche du temps perdu.* He behaves like a botanist who, having discovered a new plant, studies it progressively down to its tiniest rootlets in order to understand its origins. Thus we have the childhood of Christmas, his education, the sources of his complexes, and his crime. Act three: the story recommences where the first act

---

[12] Hartwick, p. 164.

left off and proceeds as logically as is possible toward the denouement.

I foresee this objection: What is the point of having in the denouement the pages in which Doc Hines, his wife, and Byron, like a grim chorus of three voices, tell the pastor the story of Christmas' birth? The answer to that question is found in the most original side of the technique of Faulkner—his conception of reality and of time.

The realism of William Faulkner is essentially subjective. For him an event exists only through our representation of it to ourselves. Reality, if such it is to be, must pass through the filter of our unconscious minds. Hence one can easily understand the importance of interior monologue in Faulkner's art. He used it exclusively in *As I Lay Dying.* He achieved his greatest effects with it in *The Sound and the Fury;* and if in *Light in August* we find stories directly told, the principal scenes are for the most part seen and interpreted by the witnesses or the actors of the drama. And so he had to wait until the moment when Doc Hines and his wife felt compelled to appear in order to give us the story of the early years of Christmas, who had long existed in their minds only as a memory.

Mr. Faulkner is all the less hesitant to use this technique in that it serves to illustrate his conception of time. Like J. W. Dunne, who maintains, in *An Experiment With Time,* that the present, the past, and the future coexist, even though we live only in the present, William Faulkner regards this tripartite division as no more than a convenient illusion in our brains. If, for one reason or another—old age, madness—the brain ceases to function according to the habitual pattern, our accustomed notion of time disappears and the coexistence is restored. Thus Mrs. Hines is no longer aware that Lena Grove is not Milly, and she persists in speaking of Joe as the child her grandson was thirty years ago. Mr. Faulkner, then, finds precious assistants among the demented and weak-minded. He likes them as we like all those who prove that we are right. The greatest difficulty in *The Sound and the Fury* comes from the fact that the first part is told through the brain of an idiot, Benjy, who mixes up not only the chronology of events but also names, thus confusing his niece with his brother who has been dead for eighteen years, because they are both named Quentin.

Furthermore, William Faulkner does not believe in the intrinsic value of words. "I don't claim that words have life in themselves," says Fairchild in *Mosquitoes*. "But words brought into a happy conjunction produce something that lives. . . ."[13] Addie, in *As I Lay Dying*, is Mr. Faulkner's interpreter when she says, "That was when I learned that words are no good; that words dont ever fit even what they are trying to say at."[14] A proper name, consequently, will never have a meaning in itself. This same Addie thinks of her husband's name, Anse, as a vessel until she can see Anse "liquefy and flow into it like cold molasses flowing out of the darkness into the vessel, until the jar stood full and motionless. . . ."[15] Speaking of her children Cash and Darl, she adds, "It doesn't matter what they call them." Hence it is not for the mere purpose of confusing the reader that Faulkner calls the uncle and the niece Quentin, (*The Sound and the Fury*), the father and the son Jason ("That Evening Sun"), the mother and the daughter Belle (*Sanctuary*), and that he gives the waitress the masculine first name of Bobbie.

If words have only a relative value, it is clear that they cannot enable us to penetrate to the deepest knowledge of things. Only intuition can perform that service for us. This mysterious sense of divination is particularly acute in persons whose brains emit, with difficulty, only rudimentary thoughts—the Lena Groves, the Byron Bunches. Their language, made of fragments and stammerings, arises, as Montaigne says, "from

---

[13] *Mosquitoes*, (New York: Liveright, 1927), p. 210.
[14] *As I Lay Dying*, p. 163.
[15] *Ibid.*, p. 165.

shadowy hints that they get from a few crude conceptions which they cannot sort out and clarify in their own minds and which, consequently, they cannot express. They themselves do not yet know what they mean."[16] Enigmatic by nature, these characters, with whom Faulkner sometimes achieves his greatest effects, cast, in the light of a realism that is sometimes very raw, the kind of reflections of unreality beloved by the Symbolists. They seem to say with Mélisande, "I do not understand what I am saying either, you see. . . . I do not know what I am saying. . . . I do not know what I know. . . . I no longer say what I wish. . . ."[17] And this imprecision accounts for much in the bad-dream atmosphere that emerges from Faulkner's novels. The author of *Sanctuary* is not ignorant of the power of the unexpressed. He knows also the magical charm which can emanate from a landscape, from nature at certain hours. He acknowledges the influence of these imponderables by choosing such titles for his stories as "Dry September" or *Light in August*. His descriptions brim with sensuality and are spiced with poetic symbols which would provide an abundant harvest for psychoanalysts. He knows the secrets of odors, of sounds, and of colors, just as he knows the secrets of human feelings. The odor of jasmine and the dying glimmers of the stained-glass windows are, for Miss Jenny, her whole past and her ancestral glory ("There Was a Queen"). It is because the crickets sang that Christmas can move about in an "island of silence"[18]; likewise Vardaman senses the emptiness of the square after a cow has stopped lowing there (*As I Lay Dying*).[19] So many powerful suggestions and subtle notations prove that Mr. Faulkner is more than a skillful technican, that he is a great artist.

He is also—and this is rarer—a sincere writer, without any

[16] Trans. from Montaigne, *Essais* (Paris: Gallimard, 1950), Bk. I, Chap. XXVI, p. 204.
[17] Maurice Maeterlinck, *Pélléas et Mélisande*, act. 5, sc. 2.
[18] *Light in August*, p. 216.
[19] *As I Lay Dying*, p. 241.

trace of that "romantic agony" studied by Mr. Mario Praz. If it sometimes happens that he makes our hair stand on end, it is never for the sake of effect, in the manner of a macabre joker; nor is it in obedience to a decadent aesthetic; rather it is in the manner of artists of the Middle Ages who, bent beneath the yoke of the Church and dominated by the idea of sin, painted the dance of death, sculptured faces out of nightmares, and imagined—in order to mortify the flesh—monstrous couplings.

PREFACE TO

*THE SOUND AND THE FURY**

"This novel began as a short story," William Faulkner once said to me. "It struck me that it would be interesting to imagine the thoughts of a group of children who were sent away from the house the day of their grandmother's funeral, their curiosity about the activity in the house, their efforts to find out what was going on, and the notions that would come into their minds. Then, to complicate the picture, I had the idea of someone who would be more than just a child, who in trying to find the answer, would not even have a normal brain to use—that is, an idiot. So Benjy was born. After that, the same thing happened to me that happens to many writers—I fell in love with one of my characters, Caddy. I loved her so much I couldn't decide to give her life just for the duration of a short story. She deserved more than that. So my novel was created, almost in spite of myself. It had no title until one day the familiar words 'the sound and the fury' came to me out of my unconscious. I adopted them immediately, without considering then that the rest of the Shakespearean quotation was as well

* From *Le Bruit et la fureur* (Paris: Gallimard, 1938) © Editions Gallimard 1938. The translation, by G.M.R., appeared first in *The Mississippi Quarterly* (Summer 1966) © 1966 Mississippi State University, and is reprinted by permission of the editors.

suited, and maybe better, to my dark story of madness and hatred."[1]

Indeed we find in *Macbeth*, act 5, scene 5, this definition of life: "It is a tale told by an idiot, full of sound and fury, signifying nothing." The first part of William Faulkner's novel is likewise told by an idiot; the entire book vibrates with sound and fury and will seem devoid of significance to those who hold that a man of letters, each time he takes up his pen, must deliver a message or serve some noble cause. Mr. Faulkner is content to open the Gates of Hell. He does not force anyone to accompany him, but those who trust him have no cause for regrets.

The drama takes place in Mississippi among the members of an old Southern family, once proud and prosperous but today sunk in wretchedness and humiliation. In this setting three generations tear one another apart: Jason Compson and his wife Caroline, née Bascomb; their daughter Candace (or Caddy) and their three sons, Quentin, Jason, and Maury (who is later called Benjamin, or Benjy, so that he will not sully the name of his uncle Maury Bascomb) ; and finally Quentin the daughter of Caddy. Thus there are two Jasons (father and son) and two Quentins (uncle and niece). Attached to all these are three generations of Negroes: Dilsey and her husband, Roskus; their children, Versh, T. P., and Frony; and then Luster, son of Frony.

Caddy, willful and sensual, has taken a lover, Dalton Ames. When she discovers that she is pregnant, she accompanies her mother to French Lick, a thermal springs resort in Indiana, to find a husband. On April 25, 1910, she marries Sidney Herbert Head.

Quentin, who is morbidly linked to his sister by an incestuous (although Platonic) fondness, kills himself out of jealousy on June 2, 1910, at Harvard, where he has come to study. A year

---

[1] This quotation from Faulkner was never written down in English; the version given here is an attempt to approximate his idiom.

later Caddy, cast off by her husband, abandons to her parents the baby girl to whom she has recently given birth and whom, in memory of her brother, she has named Quentin.

Then comes the death of the father, who founders in alcoholism, leaving his destitute wife with their two surviving sons, Jason and Benjamin, and the baby that Caddy no longer has permission even to see. Jason is a monster of deceit and sadism; Benjamin is an idiot. One day, having escaped from the yard, he attempted to violate a young girl. To prevent further such incidents, he was castrated. Completely harmless ever since, he wanders like an animal and expresses himself only with cries.

Quentin, Caddy's daughter, has grown up. When *The Sound and the Fury* begins, she is seventeen and, like her mother before her, already gives herself to the young men of the town. Her uncle Jason besets her with his hatred, and that is really the whole subject of the book, the hatred of Jason during the three days of April 6, 7, and 8, 1928.

Readers familiar with Faulkner's usual technique will suspect already that the author is going to shuffle the chronology to some extent. And in fact the first part takes place on April 7, 1928; the second, eighteen years earlier, on June 2, 1910; the third, on April 6, 1928; and the fourth, two days later, on April 8. As for the events, present or past, they reach us through interior monologues, the last part alone being a direct narrative in which, accordingly, there are physical descriptions of the characters (Caroline Compson, Jason, Dilsey, Benjy) whose natures have been revealed to us little by little in the course of the monologues of the three preceding parts.

To make this complex work easily accessible to the reader, I would now like to analyze in some detail Mr. Faulkner's methods of writing and to show, by bringing them into relief, how the principal difficulties can be approached and resolved. Reading William Faulkner is in itself a little science.

The structure of *The Sound and the Fury* is essentially musical. Like a composer, Faulkner uses the system of themes.

There is not, as in a fugue, a simple theme which develops and undergoes transformations; there are multiple themes which start out, vanish, and reappear to disappear again until the moment they sound forth in all their richness. One thinks of impressionist compositions, mysterious and chaotic on first hearing, but firmly structured beneath their confused appearance. *The Sound and the Fury* is a novel of atmosphere which suggests more than it says, a sort of *Night on Bald Mountain* penetrated by a diabolical wind in which damned souls are whirling, a cruel poem of hatred with each movement precisely characterized.

First movement—April 7, 1928. *Moderato:* "Life is a tale told by an idiot." It is through the atrophied brain of Benjy that Faulkner takes us into his hell. On his birthday Benjy is in the yard accompanied by his guardian, Luster, a young Negro of seventeen who has lost a quarter and is searching for it so that he can attend a tent show to be put on by a traveling company that evening. Benjy is thirty-three. For him nothing exists except animal sensations. Of these he has made himself a world in which he moves about without ever feeling restricted by notions of space and time. It is not by logic that he goes from one idea to another but by the random progression of his sensations which, unless they are direct (burning his hand, for example), are joined together by the process of association that may be set off by a gesture, a sound, or an odor. Thus the word *caddy,* spoken by some golf players, reawakens his memories of his lost sister and causes him to howl in agony. In the same way, when he snags his clothing on a fence nail, he suddenly plunges into the past to the day when, as a mere child, he got caught in a similar manner as he and Caddy were carrying a love note from Maury, their uncle, to Mrs. Patterson. By means of such retrospective soundings, two series of events materialize little by little: the grandmother's funeral, when Caddy was seven; and Caddy's wedding (April 25, 1910). Thus, in the wake of Benjy, Mr. Faulkner conducts three lines of action simultaneously.

Moreover, this tinseling of ideas free of all subservience to logic provides William Faulkner with the most suitable means of introducing the themes which will run through his symphony from one end to the other (visits to the cemetery, castration, Caddy's misconduct, the father's drunkenness, Jason's brutality, Quentin's rendezvous and her escape out the window, etc.). Embryonic in this first part, and rightly so since they are conceived in the brain of an idiot, these themes are stated precisely later on, although some of them do not reach full clarity until the last pages. At times they are presaged by a few enigmatic, one could say furtive, words. One must remember these words and wait until they reappear in sentences that give them an exact meaning. William Faulkner offers us many riddles, but he never forgets to provide the solution to them. At most, readers in a hurry will find that he makes them wait too long, and bad sportsmen will grow angry.

Second movement—June 2, 1910. This is the painful *Adagio*, the interior monologue of Quentin Compson on the day of his suicide at Harvard. Here it is no longer idiocy that disturbs the harmonious balance of thought, but the half-madness of a brain obsessed by ideas of incest and of suicide, by unbearable jealousy, by hatred for schoolmates such as Gerald Bland, a snob and a rake whom Quentin envies because love is for him a source of joy rather than an instrument of torture. The themes appear, likewise formless at first, for they are hideous thoughts held in terror by the brain that conceives them and stifles them at birth (the marriage of his too-beloved sister, the flatirons that Quentin will fasten to his feet to assure his death, the inexorable march of time which he attempts to avert by smashing his watch, and the attraction of the water which seems to lie in wait for him everywhere during the course of his last walk).

Third movement—April 6, 1928. *Allegro:* The interior monologue of Jason who, having discovered that his niece, Quentin, has arranged a rendezvous with one of the actors of the traveling company, attempts to confine her and thus drives her to the nocturnal flight that Luster and Benjy witnessed in the first part. Through the hateful mind of Jason a whole segment of the past becomes clear: the father's death, bankruptcy of the family, Caddy's misconduct and the harshness of her own people toward her, Benjy's attempt at rape which brought about his castration—all this mingled with the events of the day in the hardware store where Jason earns his living against his will.

Fourth movement—April 8, 1928. This time the narrative has become direct and objective. It begins with an *Allegro furioso*. Quentin, when she fled, carried off three thousand dollars that her uncle had appropriated for himself—hence the distraught pursuit which is abruptly interrupted by Jason's migraine and by the blow that he receives on the head. Contrastingly, next comes the *Andante religioso*, the service in the Negro church on Easter Sunday, followed, almost without transition, by an *Allegro barbaro* which ends in the calm of a *Lento*: "The broken flower drooped over Ben's fist and his eyes were empty and blue and serene again as cornice and façade flowed smoothly once more from left to right; post and tree, window and doorway, and signboard, each in its ordered place."

Such is the structural pattern of this demoniac symphony which lacks only the gaiety of a scherzo, and which achieves unity through the help of two elements of equal effectiveness— the cries of Benjy and the noble figure of Dilsey. The cries, which range from wailing to bellowing, play, in Mr. Faulkner's orchestra, the role of percussion instruments with an obsessive rhythm. This is the sonant climate of the novel. The backdrop is the Negroes, resigned witnesses of the extravagances of the whites. Among them Dilsey, black sister of Flaubert's Félicité, is the "simple heart" in all its beauty. Her animal devotion to masters whom she does not judge and her primitive good sense make it possible for her still to hold in her old hand the tiller of this drifting ship which is the Compson house. Negroes abound in contemporary novels of the South, but none attain the moving grandeur of this woman who, not in the least idealized, is, I believe, Mr. Faulkner's most successful creation.

The structure of *The Sound and the Fury* would in itself be enough to discourage the lazy reader.[2] Yet this is not the greatest of the difficulties. William Faulkner knows all the secrets of verbal alchemy. Did not Arnold Bennett say that he wrote like an angel? He knows also the power of the unexpressed. Consequently his style is full of snares. I will mention simply his very curious use of pronouns for which he only rarely gives antecedents (it is always *he* or *she,* without further specification), his use of symbols, and the boldness of his ellipses.

It is particularly in connection with Benjy that symbolism appears. For Benjy, who is more like an animal than a man, nothing exists other than sensation. Endowed with prescience, like dogs that howl in the presence of death or birds that fly before an approaching storm, he "feels" the events that take place around him and that he does not otherwise understand. Incapable of conceiving abstractions, he transcribes them into sensual images. Caddy, still a virgin, "smells like trees." After she has given herself to Dalton Ames, she no longer smells like trees, and Benjy cries, for anything that changes his habits frightens him (hence his bellowing when, on the way to the cemetery, Luster leads him to the left of the monument whereas T. P. habitually has taken him to the right). And on Caddy's wedding day he pushes her to the bathroom and forces her to enter, for that is where the lustral water flows from which she would emerge in her aboreal freshness. And Caddy, who understands, hides her face in her arms.

When Benjy is happy he speaks to us of luminous circles

---

[2] In his latest novel, *Eyeless in Gaza* (published in French under the title *La Paix des profondeurs*), Aldous Huxley goes even farther than Faulkner in the overthrow of chronology; and he does not even offer his reader the aid of associative processes. M.E.C.

which whirl more or less rapidly according to the intensity of his happiness. This is what happens when he sees fire, when he chases little girls, and, at Caddy's wedding, when he has drunk too much champagne. Mr. Faulkner is careful not to clarify these symbols, for he intends them to be somewhat indistinct like the impressions that they translate, and he does not want his readers to understand too easily a character who does not understand himself.

As for the ellipses, they are either sentence fragments which reproduce photographically, if I may put it thus, the flashing play of thought, or ideas in juxtaposition with no indication of the transitions which normally would link them together. The reader will find an excellent example of the first type on page 174. Quentin, a victim of insomnia, has gone in the darkness to the bathroom to drink a glass of water. Here is how this passage should be read: "*my* hands can see, *my* fingers *are* cooled by the invisible swan-throat where Moses' rod is not needed *to make the water spring forth. Where is* the glass? *I will have to* feel for it. Careful not *to knock it off the shelf. . . .*"[3]

Now let us take an example of the second type. Annoyed by swarming sparrows, Jason says that they ought to be poisoned: "If they'd just put a little poison out there in the square, they'd get rid of them in a day, because if a merchant cant keep his stock from running around the square, he'd better try to deal in something besides chickens, something that dont eat. . . ."[4] Here Jason, after expressing an idea, answers an objection that an interlocutor might have thought of but that remains understood (in poisoning the sparrows, they would run the risk of poisoning also the animals that were brought to the square on market days).

[3] Faulkner's exact words: "*. . . hands can see cooling fingers invisible swan-throat where less than Moses rod the glass touch tentative not to. . . ."* *The Sound and the Fury* (New York: Jonathan Cape and Harrison Smith, 1929), p. 216.
[4] *Ibid.,* pp. 309–10.

Numerous difficulties of this type present themselves and demand the sustained attention of the reader, who must, moreover, become accustomed to the inversion of dates and the confusion of similar names (the two Jasons and the two Quentins). I do not hesitate, nevertheless, to affirm that it is not at all necessary to understand every phrase completely in order to savor *The Sound and the Fury*. I would compare this novel to landscapes that improve when seen through an enveloping haze. Its tragic beauty is increased, and its mysteriousness casts a veil over horrors that would lose some of their power if seen in too much direct light. The mind that is contemplative enough to grasp, on a first reading, the meaning of all the enigmas that Faulkner offers us would undoubtedly not experience the impression of conjuration which gives this unique work its greatest charm and its genuine originality.

* * * * * *

Written when the author was beset with personal problems,[5] *The Sound and the Fury* was published in 1929. This date marks the beginning of William Faulkner's reputation in America. I mean his reputation in the intellectual milieux, for it was not until the appearance of *Sanctuary* (1931) that the general public stirred from its torpor. *The Sound and the Fury* cannot fail to arouse objections. Some minds like easy pleasures. But I believe that this novel is unanimously regarded as Mr. Faulkner's masterwork—first, because of its intrinsic value, but also because of its radiant energy. It seems that sparks fly from it unceasingly to light new fires. In *These Thirteen* (1931) one of the stories, "That Evening Sun,"[6] is composed of an episode

---

[5] Profound emotional shocks are a powerful factor in William Faulkner's inspiration. It was after the death of one of his children that he wrote *Light in August*, and *Absalom, Absalom!* was composed during the weeks following the death of one of his brothers in an airplane accident. M.E.C.

[6] A French translation of this short story was published under my name in *Europe* (January 15, 1935). M.E.C.

in the childhood of Caddy and her brothers. *Absalom, Absalom!* is partly narrated by Jason Compson and by his son Quentin, who confides in Shreve, his friend and roommate at Harvard. *The Sound and the Fury*, then, seems to be the matrix of that "human comedy" on which Mr. Faulkner is laboring diligently. To accommodate this work he has already created towns which he has mapped on the last page of *Absalom, Absalom!*

Although perfectly conscious of the inevitable imperfection in the translation of such a perilous work, I believe I can assure the French public that this is truly a translation which I offer them and not a more or less free adaptation. I have scrupulously respected the design of the original and have not, to my knowledge, added in any way to the obscurity. On the contrary, the precision of the French language has often led me, in spite of myself, to clarify the text. Having had the pleasure of listening to Mr. Faulkner give me his own comments on the most obscure points of his novel, I have not shied away from any obstacle. I have, however, resolutely set aside all efforts to carry over into my text the flavor of Negro dialect. A solution to that problem is, in my opinion, as clearly impossible as it would be for a translator working in English to reproduce the dialect of Marseille. This sacrifice granted, I hope that I have retained, in the present version, everything that contributes to the perplexing enchantment and the power of a book which has already become a landmark in the history of American literature.

PREFACE TO

*THE WILD PALMS**

The Wild Palms was published in 1939, one year after *The Unvanquished* had inaugurated a series of works in which William Faulkner, breaking away from a too strict concern with formal unity as it is ordinarily understood, proceeded to construct his novels by bringing together materials from one place and another—a practice which resulted in a misleading appearance of gratuitous artificiality. It was thus that he constructed *The Hamlet* (1940), *Knight's Gambit* (1949), and *Requiem for a Nun* (1951). In these books the author made use of stories previously published in magazines and sometimes linked by the presence of a central character, along with unpublished fragments that he carefully revised (the beginning of *The Hamlet*, "The Long Summer," is the new version of a burlesque story, "The Afternoon of a Cow," which Faulkner wrote in 1937 under the pseudonym of Ernest V. Trueblood, amusing himself by parodying his own style[1]). His resources seem inexhaustible. In *Requiem for a Nun*, for example, three

---

* From *Les Palmiers sauvages* (Paris: Gallimard, 1952) © Editions Gallimard 1952. Translation by Thomas McHaney and G.M.R.

[1] This parody was first published in a French translation: "L'Après-midi d'une vache," trans. Maurice Edgar Coindreau, *Fontaine* (June–July 1943), pp. 66–81. The original English version was published afterwards in *Furioso*, II (Summer 1947).

stories serve as backdrop for a drama which resurrects the horrors of *Sanctuary*. But of all the composite novels *The Wild Palms* is perhaps the one whose method of construction is, at first glance, the most disconcerting.

The majority of American critics (to say nothing of the public) still affirm that between the two sections, "Wild Palms" and "Old Man," no true connection exists. Malcolm Cowley himself, generally quite expert in Faulknerian matters, writes in his excellent anthology, *The Portable Faulkner:* "[In *The Wild Palms*] Faulkner had tried the experiment of writing two unrelated stories of about the same length, cutting each of them into five parts, and printing the parts alternately. . . . What he gained was an effect of contrast or counterpoint: in 'The Wild Palms' [*sic*], a man sacrificed everything for freedom and love, and lost them both; in 'Old Man,' the convict sacrificed everything to escape from freedom and love and return to the womanless security of the state prison farm." This opinion, which only a hasty reading could justify, is not borne out by a close examination of the text. Moreover, the deliberately arbitrary entanglement of two stories for the simple pleasure of playing with antitheses would scarcely represent Faulkner's usual practice. He is an artist too much like the great primordial creators for one to find the secret of his obscurities in a twisted intellectualism, in a species of counterfeiting. His obscurities are the children of the unconscious, and it would be futile to pretend to track them down in another domain. Irving Howe, in a very good study entitled "William Faulkner and the Quest for Freedom,"[2] has indeed perceived that in *The Wild Palms* there is very much more than the simple antithesis noted by Mr. Cowley. He has limited himself, however, to comments that are too superficial to be very fruitful. Each of the two stories, he says, starts with an escape only to end in an imprisonment. In each case, freedom is impossible. Money and

[2] *Tomorrow*, IX (December 1949), pp. 54–56.

respectability, among other forms of pressure exerted by Society, nullify Harry's efforts to enjoy an unfettered love worthy of the most beautiful romantic dreams. As for the convict, it is the guards, the police, the guns, and his own prison garb that tend to thwart his desire to return, after accomplishing his task, to the prison which he had only reluctantly left. In the first story, Society does its best to drive a man to his ruin; in the second, it does everything possible to keep its old victim from recovering a happiness which he had managed to enjoy despite Society. For both men, it comes to the same thing. Society has mobilized all its forces to prevent the convict from showing himself worthy of the confidence the guards have placed in him; and, after convincing Wilbourne of the vanity of his dreams, it has driven him to commit a crime against nature, a crime that Society endorses and regulates, that sometimes becomes inevitable, and that in any case is committed every day. Harry and the convict can therefore arrive at the same conclusion: for man condemned to live in contemporary Society, freedom has no meaning.

Air and water provide us with other correspondences which, though they are less generally perceived because less evident, touch upon infinitely more instructive mysteries. Air and water play integral parts in the two stories, the former passive, the latter active. Because Charlotte and Harry are already defeated, the wind, in the "Wild Palms" section, is confined to the role of witness. It illustrates and in its fury underlines with cruel irony the guilt of the two lovers. Thus a "touch with the blade to let the air in"[3] takes on a symbolic meaning unsuspected by those readers who did not fail to note that Faulkner appears to show astonishing ignorance concerning abortion. But actually, rather than strive for the accuracy of a detail, he chooses to draw upon the resources of the subconscious. Wilbourne's blasphemy (he takes the name of the air in vain) suffices to unleash

---

[3] *The Wild Palms* (New York: Random House, 1939), p. 192.

the outraged element in all its primal force. As Charlotte lies dying, the wind whistles and whirls repetitiously around the house, grandiosely seeking an interstice, a slit through which to penetrate. For her the wind is vengeance, a kind of macabre joke, and it is not by accident that Faulkner, in describing the voice of the storm, uses the words *risible* and *jeering*.

Like Harry himself, like Charlotte, the palm trees struggle and thrash wildly. The investigators of the unconscious mind have informed us that a tree is a mirror in which all human emotions may be reflected. In his work *L'Air et les songes* (a study which, like his *L'Eau et les rêves* and *La Psychanalyse du feu*, contains so many indispensable keys to the comprehension of William Faulkner, that great primitive, servitor of ancient myths), Gaston Bachelard tells us: "The tossing tree, the agitated tree, the violently disturbed tree can give us images for all human passions." In front of the window of the cell in which a victorious Society has imprisoned Wilbourne, a palm tree stands straight, not only a symbol of rectitude and strength (and thus a constant ironic example of what the unfortunate prisoner could not be), but also, through the clashing of its fronds, interpreter of the last agonies of the culprit before his acceptance of painful memory, of grief, finally brings him peace and resignation. Regarding a tree in a tempest, G. Bachelard tells us further: "Our being vibrates with a primitive sympathy. We understand that suffering is in the cosmos, that strife is in the elements, that the wills of beings are contrary, that repose is but an ephemeral blessing. The stricken tree puts the crowning touch on universal woe."[4]

After this insight, the liaison of Harry and Charlotte no longer looks like one of those vulgar affairs so relished by the novelists at the end of the last century. Transcending the particular, it takes on, by the fact that it upsets nature herself, a greater burden of meaning. Nevertheless, it remains sufficiently

---

[4] *L'Air et les songes* (Paris: Corti, 1943), p. 247.

earthbound for one to continue speaking of the story as realism. But if Faulkner is willing to consider a world the very idea of which makes him recoil in horror, he does so because it provides a springboard which enables him to reach more easily that region where the prophets spoke and the ancient bards sang. Starting with a story of carnal love in "Wild Palms," he proceeds in "Old Man" to recount the same drama but in the heroic mode—at one stroke revealing to us its primary significance without concealing any part of its full dimensions.

Faulkner's true domain is that of the eternal myths, particularly those popularized by the Bible. The themes that he prefers, his favorite images and metaphors, are those which ornament the fabric of the Old Testament, and it is indeed unjust to reproach Faulkner for scenes of violence and indecency when we accept such things in Holy Writ without blinking an eye. In "Old Man" he has given us his Deluge. It is all there: the apocalyptic vision of the rushing waters, the earth engulfed, carcasses swept along with the flotsam. Nor does he forget the monsters, those atavistic creatures—leviathans, dragons, sea serpents—which are common to all the cosmogonies and which still appear to us in our deepest dreams and are found even in our fairy tales. Of a similar order is the great wave which Faulkner twice describes as one of those terrifying archetypes. The wave closes in: "It reared, stooping; the crest of it swirled like the mane of a galloping horse and, phosphorescent too, fretted and flickered like fire."[5] Again, it is "a volume of moving water toppling forward, its crest frothed and shredded like fangs."[6] Surely we would be justified in believing that we are far from the passionate love of Harry and Charlotte. And yet beneath the seeming antitheses, that passion is still the central concern, for amidst these furious events a lone couple struggles, a woman and a man thrown together by Fate for its own sadistic amusement. The woman, like Charlotte, is pregnant, but how differ-

[5] *The Wild Palms*, p. 156.
[6] *Ibid.*, p. 171.

ent she is! An anonymous creature of instinct like Lena Grove of *Light in August* and the Negro Dilsey of *The Sound and the Fury,* she is worlds away from Charlotte, the artist who runs with the snobs and would-be bohemians Faulkner satirized in 1927 in his second novel, *Mosquitoes.* The man is an uneducated convict, led astray in adolescence but saved from irredeemable corruption by a providential imprisonment for a crime that must be blamed on Society itself. Both the man and the woman are "savages" of the type that Baudelaire defined and admired in "New Notes on Edgar Poe":

The key to the question is what we mean by the word "savage." No philosopher will dare to propose as models those vile and wretched hordes, victims of the elements, prey of the wild beasts, as incapable of constructing arms as they are of conceiving an idea of a supreme power. But if one wishes to compare modern man, civilized man, with savage man, or rather a so-called civilized nation with a so-called savage nation—that is to say, deprived of all the ingenious inventions which have made individual heroism unnecessary—who does not see that all the honor goes to the savage? By his nature, as well as by necessity, he is encyclopedic, while civilized man finds himself confined to extremely small areas of specialization. Civilized man invents the philosophy of progress in order to console himself for his abdication and forfeiture, while savage man, a dreaded and respected husband, a warrior compelled to personal bravery, a poet of the melancholy hours when the setting sun moves him to sing of the past and of his ancestors, borders much more closely on the ideal. . . . Shall we compare our torpid eyes and our deafened ears to those eyes which pierce the mists, to those ears which hear the grass growing? And the savage woman, with her simple and childlike soul, an obedient and winsome animal, who gives herself entirely, knowing that she is but half of a destiny—shall we declare her inferior to the American woman whom M. Bellegarigue (editor of *The Grocery Gazette!*) thought he was praising when he said that she was the epitome of the kept woman?

If Faulkner has not gone quite so far as to make his savage woman "an obedient and winsome animal," at least he reproduces the spirit of this declaration when he writes: ". . . man alone of all creatures deliberately atrophies his natural senses and that only at the expense of others . . . the four-legged animal gains all its information through smelling and seeing and hearing and distrusts all else while the two-legged one believes only what it reads."[7]

Henceforth we can understand why the two couples in completely similar circumstances, as we shall soon see, behave in diametrically opposite fashion. The fates of the two men, regardless of appearances, are no less opposed. While Charlotte—the "American woman"—strives to suppress life and drags her lover along with her into crime, the savage woman aspires only to give birth to her baby. She who breaks the natural law dies of an operation which, in principle, should have succeeded; conversely, the savage woman giving birth (performing woman's natural role) under the most frightful conditions becomes in a manner invulnerable. In the middle of an island infested with snakes she brings a vigorous child into the world, and the tin can with the jagged edges does not lead to any of the mortal complications which are caused by the sterilized blade. This detail, which many have singled out (as they did the corncob in *Sanctuary*) as the mark of a morbid and perverted imagination, is not without profound resonance, and I do not hesitate to suggest that if William Faulkner took some liberty with surgical fact, he did so not solely for the purpose of arousing the fury of the wind but also because he deemed it necessary, in order to strengthen his demonstration, in both cases to make use of a cutting edge.

Without pretending to note all the contrasting details which serve as counterpoint in the plaited themes of *The Wild Palms,* let us approach now the great basic antithesis—the unyielding tenacity of the convict contrasted with the passivity of Wilbourne, who, shaken by an emotional storm comparable to the flood, reasons, discusses, argues, and understands, but sinks deeper each day into an impotent softness. Park benches and

[7] *Ibid.,* p. 105.

long solitary walks (artifices by which the timid win compen-
satory victories over a terrifying world) are his only defense
against an adverse fate. The convict, on the other hand, understands nothing. He does not even know where he is. When he
thinks he is going forward, he is going backward. If he raises his
head, it is only to receive a blow whose source he cannot determine. He huddles in the bottom of the boat, wipes away the
blood which covers his face, and sets out again. Nothing can
daunt his courage or his endurance. He is indeed Baudelaire's
"warrior compelled to personal bravery." He never compro-
mises. Aware of the harm which Society and its falsehoods
have done him, he remains suspicious and aloof. In this way
an animal avoids what has once caused it pain. Taught by experience the danger of firearms (weapons *par excellence* of
civilized man), when he hunts alligators he prefers, as did his
distant ancestors, to rely on the strength of his biceps and on
the knife, which he has been accustomed to use in slaughtering
pigs. With the infinite patience of prehistoric man he whittles
and shapes the log which, in order to continue the struggle, he
must make into a paddle. Five or six times Society dangerously
reminds him of its existence. Guns crack, a drink of whiskey
awakens his dormant violence, and there is trouble over a married woman who is scarcely better than the girl whose ambition
was to make him a high class gangster so that he could maintain her regally. He escapes these snares just as he escapes the
great wave. Finally he is allowed to regain his refuge—the
penitentiary, a kind of Alceste's desert where he can again
find order, peace and security, his plow and his mule, and his
cronies, to whom, while rolling his cigarette with a sure hand,
he recounts his odyssey. Ten years later Harry Wilbourne, behind the bars of his prison, shreds between his trembling fingers
the tobacco that he does not know how to handle. Emasculated
by the dominating false values which the modern world has set
up as dogmas, he also has chosen captivity, but it is as a refuge
to shelter his fear, a tomb where he may weep over his errors.

Nature bends with love over those who have remained close to her, and the penitentiary is the most beautiful of repayments for the convict—a return to "that monastic existence of shotguns and shackles where he would be secure. . . ."[8] Henceforth his life is assured, for only the savages who know how to endure without complaint are worthy of survival. The others, the Charlottes and Harrys, sons and daughters of a degenerate world where if Christ returned it would be necessary to crucify him again, where if Venus reappeared "she would be a soiled man in a subway lavatory with a palm full of French post-cards"[9]— their days are numbered. In the midst of their confusion, they no longer know (as primitive man knows by instinct) that the swimming deer leads the way to the safety of the firm ground of an island more surely than all the moral systems and the philosophies, products of man's intelligence. It is also a deer which, by the gracefulness of its bounding, makes Charlotte understand, on the day she regains contact with the primitive soil, something which neither school nor atelier, much less the cocktail parties of the avant-garde, have taught her—that is, the goal which she should seek in her art. "Nature is a gentle guide," Montaigne said long ago, "but no more gentle than prudent and just."

It remains for us only to bring out, as we have done for the wind in Harry's drama, the symbolic value of the flood in the drama of the convict. I shall merely touch upon the subject; one could hardly treat it in depth within the limited scope of a preface. Let us take as our Ariadne's thread a page from Jung's *L'Homme à la découverte de son âme:*

If the collective equality of the psyche were not a primordial fact, the origin and matrix of all individual psyches, it would be a gigantic illusion. But despite our individual consciousness it unquestionably continues to exist as the *collective unconscious*—the sea upon which the

---

[8] *Ibid.*, p. 153.
[9] *Ibid.*, p. 136.

ego rides like a ship. For this reason also, nothing of the primordial world of the psyche has ever been lost. Just as the sea stretches its broad tongues between the continents and laps them round like islands, so our original unconsciousness presses round our individual consciousness. In the catastrophe of mental disease the storm-tide of the sea surges over the island and swallows it back into the depths. In neurotic disturbances there is at least a bursting of dikes, and the fruitful lowlands are laid waste by flood. Neurotics are all shore-dwellers— they are the most exposed to the dangers of the sea. So-called normal people live inland, on higher, drier ground, near placid lakes and streams. No flood however high reaches them, and the circumambient sea is so far away that they even deny its existence.[10]

This passage enlarges our horizons to a singular extent. The fierce struggle of the convict and the ordeal of the woman during the search for an island where she can bring forth new life and regain a measure of stability, have become the drama of the individual consciousness "surrounded by the treacherous sea of the unconscious."[11] The dikes are broken. The "turbid Maelstorms, the cataracting gulfs" of Rimbaud's *Bateau Ivre* lie in wait for their prey. He who has not betrayed Nature and has not worshipped false gods regains—like the wild beast—the high ground where he will be able to survive and succeed in denying the existence of the sea. The other one, whose nerves are shattered by the power of a pernicious civilization, will always be confronted by this sea; and the clashing palms just outside the bars of his cell will insure that fear and suffering will never abandon him. The drama of Harry, like that of the convict, is the drama of shipwreck. Harry also

[10] C. G. Jung, *L'Homme à la découverte de son âme* (Geneva: Editions du Mont-Blanc, 1950), p. 39. This volume is not to be confused with *Modern Man in Search of a Soul* (New York, 1933), which is a different collection of essays. The essay from which Coindreau quotes was first published as "Die Bedeutung der Psychologie für die Gegenwart," *Wirklichkeit der Seele* (Zurich, 1934). The English translation is by R. F. C. Hull and is quoted by permission of Princeton University Press from "The Meaning of Psychology for Modern Man," *The Collected Works of C. G. Jung*, Vol. X, *Civilization in Transition*, ed. Herbert Read et al. (New York, 1964), pp. 137–38.
[11] Jung, *Civilization in Transition*, p. 138.

sails on waters which at the outset were calm but heavy with menace. William Faulkner made this quite clear. The morning of his twenty-seventh birthday Harry "looked down his body toward his foreshortened feet and it seemed to him that he saw the twenty-seven irrevocable years diminished and foreshortened beyond them in turn, as if his life were to lie passively on his back as though he floated effortless and without volition upon an unreturning stream."[12] Peaceful waters, still feminine; but they will become virile later when passion rouses in them "a fury," writes Gaston Bachelard in *L'Eau et les rêves,* which "man is quick to boast that he can subdue. Thus violent water is soon met with violence. A duel of spitefulness begins between man and the flood. The water assumes a rancor, it changes sex. In becoming evil it becomes masculine."[13] Man then finds himself faced with an adversary worthy of him—Old Man, terrible but faithful, at the height of one of his periodic fecundating debauches. The waters which the convict despises are the little streams, the piddling creeks which run now in one direction, now in another, with all the inconsistent frivolity of woman. Charlotte herself has the bisexuality of water. Certainly she is a woman, but Harry can see the masculine in her, too. He remains the frightened bird, she the hawk who fears nothing. Over and over Faulkner emphasizes that Charlotte is indeed more of a man than her lover. It is not without reason that he gives her a taste for sculpture, the most masculine of arts, if we once again accept the conclusions of G. Bachelard. "In the modeling of clay," he says, "we find a kind of work which gives rise to reverie in accord with an especially powerful will, with the male joy of penetrating into the substance, of touching the inner matter, of conquering earth intimately as water conquers earth, of taking part in the combat of the elements, of sharing a power that dissolves things irremediably." The Old Man, himself a sculptor, finds in the

---

[12] *The Wild Palms,* pp. 33–34.
[13] *L'Eau et les rêves,* (Paris: Corti, 1942), p. 21.

convict an adversary whom nothing can strike down. Charlotte, in the erotic turmoil through which she drags Harry, partaking at once of the femininity of the unpredictable streams and the forthright brutality of the river, finds herself face to face with only a timorous sparrow.

The two sections of *The Wild Palms*, then, illuminate each other, and without their alternation the deepest meaning of each would remain concealed. But this meaning is the only one which matters. To say that "Old Man" gains by being printed and read independently of "Wild Palms" is to pretend that a fugue would be more beautiful if the answer and the countersubject were detached from the subject. I realize that the separation of the two stories makes them easier to read. But if William Faulkner is occasionally obscure, he is not willfully so. His complexities, whether of content or of form, are never gratuitous. Consequently, they ought to be respected. This is why, in this French version, I have worked to reproduce scrupulously all the particulars of the writing, notably the contingent indication, immediately following the pronoun, of the name which the pronoun stands for, and the interminable parentheses, which occur in the least convenient places, thus obliging the reader to pass over an often considerable number of lines to complete the interrupted phrase. *The Wild Palms*, therefore, will be for the French reader what it was for the American reader of 1939—a novel of enigmatic construction, on the fringe of the chronicle of Jefferson and Yoknapatawpha County,[14] but conforming in all respects to the ideal the author has claimed as his, and which in his Stockholm address he reproached the young writers of today for too readily disavowing—the exclusive choice as subjects for novels of the "old verities and truths of the heart, the old universal

---

[14] "Old Man" could in a strict sense be attached to this chronicle, for on the map that William Faulkner drew for Malcolm Cowley's anthology *The Portable Faulkner* he indicates that the convict was born quite near the Old Frenchman's Place where Popeye murdered Tommy. M.E.C.

truths lacking which any story is ephemeral and doomed—love and honor and pity and pride and compassion and sacrifice . . . the problems of the human heart in conflict with itself which alone can make good writers because only that is worth writing about, worth the agony and the sweat."

WILLIAM FAULKNER:

THE NOBEL PRIZE IN

LITERATURE*

Critics, for the most part, are like childless couples. Incapable of bringing viable progeny into the world, they have no recourse except adoption. In 1930 I adopted William Faulkner. Last November 10 he received the Nobel Prize.

He was first brought to my attention by one of my students, who has since made a name for himself, James Burnham. He described Faulkner to me as a young novelist who, with modesty and discretion, wrote masterpieces that no one read because he was ignorant of the art of publicity and disdained the easy ways of playing on the emotions of the public. *As I Lay Dying* had just been published. I had not read fifty pages of this admirable book before my mind was made up. The French nation absolutely had to become acquainted with an artist of such pronounced originality. I must say that in the American academic milieux where I let my enthusiasm be known, I was looked on with a jaundiced eye. Faulkner, whose works were known to a scant handful of young intellectuals, already had the reputation of not being a writer for polite society. When *Sanctuary* appeared, this tacit disapproval became outright condemnation: Did I still dare, after this abominable narrative,

* From *France-Amérique*, November 26, 1950, © France-Amérique. Reprinted by permission of the editors. Translation by G.M.R.

to militate in favor of such a morbid, depraved novelist? And in doing so, would I not be ashamed of soiling the reputation of American letters in the eyes of the French?

I dared and I was not ashamed. June 1, 1931, I published in *La Nouvelle revue française* the first article in the French language on William Faulkner. Then, in the winter of 1932 I produced in rapid succession two translations, "Septembre ardent" in *La Nouvelle revue française* and "Une Rose pour Emilie" in *Commerce.* The reception given these two stories was most encouraging. Readers were not put off by the fact that one of them deals with a lynching and the other with an old maid who for many years spends each night beside the skeleton of her lover. They were able to appreciate the power and the supreme technical skill of the stories. At this point the house of Gallimard decided to bet on my colt. Gallimard acquired the translation rights not only for all the works already written but for all those to come, and publication soon began. While I worked on the French version of *As I Lay Dying,* Messrs. R. N. Raimbault and Henri Delgove completed a translation of *Sanctuary* for which André Malraux wrote an important preface. The latter made its appearance in 1933, a few months earlier than *Tandis que j'agonise,* which came out with an introduction by my friend Valery Larbaud. Since that time scarcely a year has passed without a new novel by Faulkner on display in the windows of French bookstores.

In 1937, the year when Messrs. Raimbault and Delgove published *Sartoris,* I spent eight days with William Faulkner, who at that time was working for a Hollywood studio. I had committed myself to an arduous task, the translation of *The Sound and the Fury,* the most complex but also perhaps the richest of Faulkner's works. With me he did not economize either his patience or his time. He was merely astonished that I should take such pains to reproduce as faithfully as possible a novel whose scope he did not seem to have calculated. And if his pride swelled at all, he unconsciously dissimulated that fact behind his genuine surprise at the success he had already achieved in France. What would he say if he knew (and I am convinced that he knows nothing of these matters) that soon after the publication of *Tandis que j'agonise* Jean-Louis Barrault produced a pantomime entitled *Autour d'une mère* adopted from the novel, if he knew that today he is the object of the philososphical meditations of M. Jean-Paul Sartre (who claims in some ways to be his disciple), that he inspires some of the subtle investigations of Mme Claude-Edmonde Magny, and others; in short, that in every sphere of French intellectual life he is placed in the highest ranks.

If he were willing to believe all this, he would not be vain about it. Lost in a universe of his own imagining, this small man aged fifty-three lives withdrawn from the world on his farm in Oxford, Mississippi. I would like for him to know that, on the other side of the ocean, his earliest friends, more vainglorious than he will ever be, those who adopted him and have believed in him for more than twenty years, feel today the proud satisfaction of parents whose son, misunderstood for too long, finally receives the prize for excellence, the most flattering of laurel crowns.

WILLIAM FAULKNER'S ART*

It is good for any kind of routine, however pleasant, to be interrupted from time to time. Consequently, I yield unhesitatingly to the various reasons that prompt me to discuss the art of William Faulkner, even though my regular readers may be somewhat astonished. Moreover, the influence of Faulkner's works on the contemporary French novel is such that to speak of them is actually not outside my province.

I admit that one of the reasons which determined me to write today about the author of *Sanctuary* is the extreme reserve—not to put it more strongly—with which the American press seems to have received the news that William Faulkner has been awarded the Nobel Prize. I expected the critics for all the important newspapers to pay him due homage immediately, if only in a few paragraphs. I thought I would see his portrait, in black and white or in color, on the covers of literary or news weeklies, as on the most insignificant occasions one sees the portraits of politicians, generals, boxers, and film stars. Of course, I do not read all the periodicals, but I must say that

* From "L'Art de William Faulkner," *France-Amérique,* December 3, 1950, © France-Amérique. Reprinted by permission of the editors. Translation by G.M.R.

until this moment I feel like Sister Anne: I wait but nothing of importance happens. A small notice, a small photograph at the bottom of a page—not much more. I do not believe I am going too far in asserting that there has been a stronger reaction in France, and I presume that pens and typewriters were not idle there the day after November 10. More precisely, I can affirm that M. Jean-Paul Sartre, with the speed of a reflex, is already preparing to publish in the next numbers of his journal *Les Temps Modernes* one of the two parts that make up *The Wild Palms*. Several works—notably *Absalom, Absalom!*—are in preparation. Their publication will be necessarily rather slow, for the translators of Faulkner are few and the work is long and difficult; at least it is if one has adopted the principle of printing nothing until he has exhausted the possibilities available in the transposition of a text from one language to another.

Faulkner's is a difficult art, and that fact accounts for much of the indifference—sometimes even the hostility—of the general public toward him. First of all there is his choice of very grim stories as subject matter. Those who reproach him most bitterly for that are usually assiduous readers of the Bible. Their sin is inconsistency, for William Faulkner, strongly influenced by the Scriptures, has invented nothing in the realm of horrors that was not already in Holy Writ, whether it be murder, rape, or incest. Why should he not be allowed to use the kind of thing that one accepts in the Old Testament without raising an eyebrow? The reason is that he manages to accentuate the dramatic element in these themes with all the means at his disposal: scenery, style, what is said, and especially what is not said or, more precisely, what is temporarily held back. For if Faulkner sometimes makes us hunt the key to his mysteries, he plays fair and always ends by giving it to us.

It is exceptional for him to go beyond the borders of his native Mississippi. There he has reserved for himself a county, Yoknapatawpha, and within that a city, Jefferson. Overwhelming heat bears down on the ruined plantations where old families, haughtily draped in the past, wait for death to put an end to their proud decrepitude. This is the South in agony but "unvanquished," to use the word under which Faulkner grouped seven of his stories in 1938. Opposite these vestiges of a past age are the newcomers, money-minded men whose essentially modern code of honor remains incompatible with the traditions of an older world. Fate weighs heavily on all these characters, no matter which side they are on, just as the hand of the gods weighs on the characters of mythology. And consequently Faulkner's novels have the same stress on ineluctability as that found in ancient drama. André Malraux understood this quite well when, in his preface to *Sanctuary*, he wrote, *"Sanctuary* marks the intrusion of Greek tragedy into the detective story."

This is how it had to be. Without this quality of permanence, of universality, how could one explain the power of Faulkner's work? If his work is, as some have said, simply that of a regionalist, how is it that his stories appeal to countries as diverse as England, France, Germany, the Scandinavian states, and the South American republics? Clearly they must contain something other than local color, than a study of regional manners. They contain, in a transposed form, the great myths, those upon which humanity has fed ever since the world began and behind which are hidden certain eternal appetites nourished by the deepest and consequently the most turbid wellsprings of our unconscious. Faulkner exteriorizes the things that swarm in the lower regions of the human soul. If they are not beautiful, we cannot properly blame him. This is especially true in view of the fact that he is the first to take offense at them, for he is a puritan, albeit in the "proper" sense of the word, as he wrote me once. To illustrate the point I will call attention only to the anathemas which he hurls at women and which seem to spring from the mouth of John the Baptist, fulminating from the bottom of his dungeon against the lascivious Salome.

He is, in other words, a moral psychologist. The game he pursues and scrutinizes with minute, unlimited patience is man. He uses the most modern techniques, notably the interior monologue, for he seems to have some sort of aversion for direct narrative. This is not surprising. Since his universe is subjective, the external world becomes real only to the extent that he perceives it through his characters. He relies on them to tell his stories unless he delves into their past himself and gradually reconstitutes it. Jean-Paul Sartre has written:

> Faulkner's vision of the world seems comparable to that of a man seated in an open car and looking backwards. At each instant, formless shadows, flutterings, vague tremblings, and a kind of confetti of light appear to the right and to the left, but only with distance do they become trees, men, and automobiles. The past takes on a kind of super-reality; its contours are firm and clear, unchangeable. The present, undefined and fleeting, is weak by comparison. It is full of holes, and the things of the past invade it through these holes—things that are fixed, immovable, silent as judges or stares. Faulkner's monologues remind us of airplane flights replete with air pockets: at each pocket the hero's consciousness "falls into the past" and then rises only to fall again. The present is not; it becomes; everything *was*.[1]

A little farther on in this essay on "Time in the Work of Faulkner" Sartre compares Faulkner with Proust, pointing out the similarities and the differences between their conceptions of time. But he does not touch on the question of style; yet that also offers material for some interesting comparisons.

Faulkner's style, in fact, is not without some obvious analogies with that of Proust. It is a poetic style, loaded and sometimes overloaded with images, interrupted by interminable incidents which follow the slow progress of thought, the meanderings of introspection and the sinuosities of analysis. Proust, however, nourished more on classical disciplines, accepts certain conventional restraints. Chronology, for example, inspires in him a respect that is unknown to Faulkner. Whereas Proust's

---

[1] Jean-Paul Sartre, "A Propos de *Le Bruit et la fureur:* La Temporalité chez Faulkner," *Situations I* (Paris: Gallimard, 1947), p. 73.

characters are highly conscious and as sensitive as reeds, Faulkner's most noteworthy ones are idiots, beings whose atrophied brains function only by the association of ideas initiated by some excitation of the senses. Thanks to them, as in *The Sound and the Fury*, Faulkner can keep several narratives going at once, though they are separated by days and sometimes by years. The story is told only in bits and starts, the "flutterings" and the "confetti of light" in Sartre's phrase. But—and this is where the artist's virtuosity shines—these bits and starts never remain as such. Always as the novel develops they find their junctures, fitting together like the pieces of a puzzle. Then the picture appears, well ordered and lifelike—a marvelous recompense for the serious reader who, having agreed to play the game, does not censure the author for the false leads and the reticence which, though retarding it, only make the reader's pleasure more savory.

WILLIAM FAULKNER

AND ERNEST HEMINGWAY*

For the second time within four years American literature has reached the pinnacle of distinction. In 1950 William Faulkner received the Nobel Prize: this year Ernest Hemingway has been chosen for that high honor. What conclusion must we draw from these two selections so close together if it is not that the creative spirit in North America is not as indigent as some would have us believe. In the realm of the novel the New World can henceforth march in the same rank as the Old.

To be sure, no more than in the case of William Faulkner, the awarding of the Nobel Prize to the author of *A Farewell to Arms* will not be greeted with unanimous applause. Young novelists, among others, will smile—all those who regard Hemingway merely as the spokesman for college students given to erotic confessions and athletic rodomontade as proof of their still uncertain virility. But the public will not say what was often said in 1950: Who is this unknown? Hemingway, in fact, has been widely read at all levels in America ever since 1926. A few books that are mediocre or downright bad, beginning with *Death in the Afternoon*, caused his stock to decline for a while; but his latest narrative, a long novella entitled *The Old*

* From *Journal de Genève*, December 13, 1954. Reprinted by permission of the editors. Translation by G.M.R.

Man and the Sea, won his public over again. In this work they found the Hemingway of old, as romantic as one could wish, a sensitive interpreter of nature, and a skillful craftsman. The enthusiastic reception of this work, in which melancholy is as adroitly managed as is sentimentality, undoubtedly had an important bearing on the decision of the judges in Stockholm. And these judges were right, for Hemingway is not a negligible author.

Having arrived on the scene at a time when the novel had sunk deep into the gray monochrome of a realism that was not without its powerful exponents (Theodore Dreiser, for example) but was usually timorous, he attacked with the somewhat blundering fervor of youth what remained of Victorian prudery in the ethics and the vocabularies of his predecessors. Amid the merciless opacities of the period he recreated the brilliance of Italian sunshine, of brooks flashing with trout, and of the Spanish toreros' scarlet *muletas.* His only means was his style, a nervous staccato style used to present characters whose actions and reflexes took the place of an interior life. Since he shattered taboos and since his books were both a healthy reaction and easy to read, his success was instantaneous and his influence undeniable not only in the United States but abroad, and expecially in France, where the novel had begun to suffer from hypertrophy of the analytic sense and from the abuse of unhealthy introspection. Consequently, his heroes were appreciated for traits which in another period would have made them detested: their cocky manner, their primitive and brutish roughness, their pride in the fact that they were absolutely devoid of thought in a century where there had been too much thinking. Only time will reveal the depth of the impression they made and enable us to judge its desirability.

In 1947 Albert Camus, although recognizing his indebtedness to Hemingway, declared in an interview with Jean Desternes that Hemingway's art "is more elementary than universal, or rather that it is universal only on the elementary level and that to put it into general use would amount to the suppression of nine-tenths of those things that give richness to art and to life."

However that may be, Hemingway was the great man in the early part of the period between the two world wars. But in Oxford, Mississippi, there lived a small, shy, solitary man who was tormented by dreams that he exorcised by writing somber stories. Completely ignorant of the techniques of self-promotion, he was still unknown when Hemingway's sun had risen to its zenith. The year 1929 witnessed the triumph of *A Farewell to Arms*. In that same year Faulkner published one of the great novels of modern times, *The Sound and the Fury*. Only an alert few read it with admiration. It took a number of long years, a half-dozen masterpieces, and—I am not afraid to say it— European consecration to bring William Faulkner the kind of fame in his own country that had gone to Hemingway's head as early as *The Sun Also Rises*. But the Tarpeian Rock is close to the Capitol. While Faulkner's star was rising, Hemingway's was setting. Little by little he became what Gertrude Stein had predicted—"a museum piece." As the wrinkles deepened, the young turned away from the god that youth had made. Soon Hemingway symbolized an epoch that was finished: the age of jazz, of prohibition, and of the Paris of Montparnasse. William Faulkner, with each new book, demonstrated more and more clearly that he was a man for all times and all places. He was never popular (in the "commercial" sense of the word) and he never will be, for his books remain hermetic. And if today he is no longer indifferent to official honors, he continues to do absolutely nothing to attract them. I would go so far as to say that he reached the highest rank in world literature without knowing it. Sweden owed it to herself to honor him first.

In crowning Hemingway second, she paid tribute to an earlier period that was not without its charm, and at the same time honored a body of fiction that is greater in its influence and its resonances than in its inherent qualities.

WILLIAM FAULKNER IN FRANCE*

It is when a literature is showing signs of lassitude that influences begin to make themselves felt. Just as a blood transfusion may save an organism threatened by anemia, new elements introduced into a weakening art form may effect its restoration. Sometimes those elements are to be found right at home. An author, who may have remained relatively obscure during his earlier years, may eventually become a guide for succeeding generations. Gide's influence, for example, really began after 1914. But however important such isolated cases may be, penetration of foreign literatures has a far more invigorating effect.

In the course of her artistic evolution, France has absorbed new blood from Italy, Spain, England, Germany, Russia, and, at various times, from the United States. In the second half of the nineteenth century, the example of Poe enabled Baudelaire to give to poetry that new quality which Hugo so appropriately termed *"un frisson nouveau."* Later, when poetry was in danger of becoming lost in the mists of a degenerated Symbolism, the younger poets turned towards Walt Whitman; the Abbaye

* First published in *Yale French Studies,* X (1953), pp. 85–91. Copyright © 1953 by *Yale French Studies.* Reprinted by permission of the editors with Coindreau's notes, essentially as they appeared in the first publication.

group renewed contact with the soil and sang the praises of the brotherhood of man and the pleasures of the good earth. The age of gladioli, swans, golden keys, was past, and the deep forests with their mysterious castles were replaced by the *villes tentaculaires.* Then came the First World War and the mad but delightful period that followed victory. France was open to all suggestions. This time it was the American novelists who were welcomed. In 1928, the publication of Dos Passos' *Manhattan Transfer* commanded the attention of both the sophisticated and the general reader. Between 1931 and 1937 works of Faulkner, Hemingway, and Caldwell appeared simultaneously. In the spring of 1939 *Des Souris et des hommes* ushered in John Steinbeck. The critics, especially the younger ones, leaned toward these newcomers. In 1938, Jean-Paul Sartre ended an essay on John Dos Passos and his novel *1919* with these words: "I consider Dos Passos the greatest writer of our time."[1] Thus began the American tidal wave which, after the Liberation, was to break upon intellectual France. Translations were published indiscriminately, and *Le Bruit et la fureur, Les Raisins de la colère* and *Autant en emporte le vent* were devoured with equal voracity. A *poncif* soon appeared: the American novel was a direct and brutal account, a series of pictures, produced by self-taught writers whose emotions were sufficiently violent to compensate for their deficiencies in technique. The young Frenchmen who had lived through the dark years of the Occupation and who had, or thought they had, something important to say, found a stimulating encouragement in these American writers; in their haste to express themselves, they accepted them unreservedly.

Questioned by Jean Desternes on the influence exercised by those contemporary American novelists, Albert Camus replied that one of the reasons for that influence lay in the fact that the technique of these novelists was a *technique de facilité*. "The

---

[1] "A Propos de John Dos Passos et de *1919*," *La Nouvelle revue française,* LI (August 1938), pp. 292–301; reprinted in *Situations I* (Paris, 1947), pp. 14–25.

novel, then, ignores all that which up to now has been considered the proper subject matter of literature, that is to say, broadly speaking, man's inner life. Man is described but is never explained or interpreted. The result is that one can write a novel simply by drawing upon his memory or upon direct observation." In other words, the novelist becomes almost indistinguishable from the reporter, and the novel is nothing more than a sort of camouflaged journalism. The value of these writings is, then, mainly documental. "The literature which we read," adds A. Camus, "is a first-rate document, but has only the remotest relation to art." The dangerous generalization of this opinion would be open to criticism if it were not for the fact that Camus took care to add parenthetically "with the exception of William Faulkner and two or three others."[2]

Certainly this judgment, though indeed quite accurate when dealing with war novels written by nerve-shattered eyewitnesses, could not have been applied to such works as *Lumière d'août;* and when Boris Vian was writing his parodies on the American *roman noir* it was not, I dare hope, of William Faulkner that he was thinking. As the years pass, time begins to lend perspective, and although the vogue for the American novel is giving signs of decreasing, the interest in William Faulkner remains unchanged. The surprise which *Sanctuaire* caused was followed by a respectful and lasting admiration, and, a few weeks ago, the critics gave as much space to *Les Palmiers sauvages* as they had given to *Tandis que j'agonise* or *Treize histoires.*

Faulkner's appearance in France dates from June 1, 1931, when I published the first article written on him in French.[3] The United States had become acquainted with him only a few months earlier. According to Robert W. Daniel, only three articles had appeared before 1930.[4] But 1931 had witnessed the

[2] *Combat,* January 17, 1947.
[3] "William Faulkner," *La Nouvelle revue française,* XXXVI (June 1931), pp. 926–30.
[4] *A Catalogue of the Writings of William Faulkner* (New Haven: Yale University Library, 1942).

appearance of *Sanctuary*, and the violence of that story had finally stirred the critics who, up to that time, had apparently been little moved by the less spectacular aspects of Faulkner's preceding novels.

During the winter of 1932 I introduced to the French public the art of Faulkner by presenting two of the best stories in *These Thirteen:* "Septembre ardent" and "Une Rose pour Emilie."[5] These were enough to launch the future Nobel Prize winner on a brilliant career in France. R. N. Raimbault and Henri Delgove undertook the translation of *Sanctuary* while I worked on that of *As I Lay Dying*. Impressed by "Une Rose pour Emily," Valery Larbaud agreed to write a preface to my translation:

My letter mail arrived later than my book mail, and so I first received a copy of *As I Lay Dying* [that is, before receiving a letter from Coindreau], which you had so kindly asked the publishers to send to me. I read it with great interest, and I shall be very pleased to write the preface to your French translation. I confess that I am awaiting the felicities of your translation in order to be sure that I understand a certain number of expressions that seemed strange to me in the text. But the dramatic interest of the work carries the reader through such difficulties. It will be compared, I think, to *The People of Podlipnoye*[6]; during these last few days while reading *As I Lay Dying* I have had the same kind of impressions that I had long ago while reading that great book. There is something very striking about the starkness of the language and the style. The characters are unforgettable.[7]

On January 1, 1933, he informed me that he had finished the preface that very morning:

Today I am happy to tell you—while sending you my best wishes for the new year—that this morning I finished the preface to your trans-

---

[5] *La Nouvelle revue française,* XXXVIII (January 1932), pp. 49–65; *Commerce,* (Winter 1932), pp. 111–37.

[6] One of the earliest (1846) realistic novels portraying peasant life, by Fyodor Mikhaylovich Reshetnikov.

[7] Unpublished letter, dated September 14, 1932.

lation of *As I Lay Dying*. . . . It was not easy to compose; for a long time I beat around the bush, writing nothing, but reading frequently either in the text or in your very precise translation, in which I have not found a single error. The most important thing was to inform the reader, to explain to him as briefly as possible both the subject and the merits of the book. I believe I have done that, and I am rather pleased with my work.[8]

A very understandable satisfaction, indeed, for Larbaud had foreseen what the future was to confirm; that is, that Faulkner is an epic poet as well as a novelist. "We can," he wrote in his preface, "without any intention of making a parody on the novel, transpose it into an episode of epic dimensions: the episode of the funeral procession of the (Homeric) queen, Addie Bundren, conducted, in accordance with her final wishes, by her husband, Anse, and by her children, the princes." This interpretation implies that, contrary to the opinion still held by some, Faulkner is not a regionalist writer but rather an artist who draws from the same sources that have always fed the great literatures of the world. It is not surprising, therefore, that Larbaud, on reading *As I Lay Dying,* should have thought of one of Reshetnikov's novels. He might well have been reminded also of Jacob Wassermann's *Christian Wahnschaffe,* where there is a funeral procession (with obstacles, accidents, and hovering vultures) which seems a kind of preliminary sketch for that of Addie Bundren.

It had first been decided that *Tandis que j'agonise* would appear before *Sanctuaire,* for which André Malraux was writing an introduction. This explains the last paragraph of Larbaud's preface: "It is hoped that the success of this version of *As I Lay Dying* will encourage the publisher to put out a translation of *Sanctuary.*" Actually, *Sanctuaire* appeared first. At the last moment it was thought that the somber story of Temple Drake, more audacious and morbid than any of the *romans noirs* published up to that time, would be more likely to excite

[8] Unpublished letter, dated January 1, 1933.

the readers than the technical complexities of *Tandis que j'agonise*.[9] *Sanctuaire* came out in 1933. In August of the same year, I published "Il Etait une reine" in the *Nouvelle revue française*.[10] *Tandis que j'agonise* came off the press in April, 1934. At the present time, the works of William Faulkner in French consist of twelve volumes (all but two printed by the Librairie Gallimard), the latest being *Les Palmiers sauvages* (February 1952) which followed by just a few months *Le Gambit du cavalier*. *L'Intrus dans la poussière* and *Requiem pour une nonne* are in preparation, as well as a collection of poems, *Le Rameau vert*.

Even a rapid study of the reactions to the principal novels of Faulkner reveals not only a diversity of approaches indicative of the richness of the subject, but an accuracy of judgments that time has but confirmed. We have seen that Valery Larbaud, sponsor and interpreter of James Joyce in France, needed only to read two books to sense Faulkner's epic quality. André Malraux, too, recognized this quality in *Sanctuaire:* "A mysterious force, at times epical, springs from his writing whenever he places a character face to face with the irremediable." It is on the notion of the "irremediable" that Malraux particularly insists. "As Lawrence is wrapped up in sexuality, Faulkner buries himself in the irremediable." In this inexorable world, an endless duel is fought—the duel between Man and Death. "One destiny stands behind all these different and similar beings, like Death over a ward for incurables." Malraux's awareness of the presence of this Fate dominating a world of crime and violence caused him to write the often quoted sentence: "*Sanctuaire* marks the intrusion of Greek tragedy into the detective story."[11]

A year before the appearance of *Tandis que j'agonise*, Eu-

[9] When, in 1936, Larbaud included his preface in *Ce Vice impuni, la lecture, domaine anglais*, he left out the last paragraph.

[10] *La Nouvelle revue française*, XLI (August 1933), pp. 213–33.

[11] Preface to *Sanctuaire*.

gène Dabit had published *Un Mort tout neuf* which he sent me in November, 1934, with this dedication: "To M. E. Coindreau, this story which will remind him—at least a little— of *Tandis que j'agonise.* With the hope that we will meet some day." The kinship between the two novels is clearly brought out in Dabit's review of Faulkner's story. "Upon reading this book," he writes, "I saw an amplification of my own adventure. It unfolded within another frame, broader and wild, under a real sky, in the torrid heat of the South; the characters that interested me were weighty, dominated by their destiny, submissive to primitive instincts which are not those of the petty French bourgeois." Further on he mentions Faulkner's realism: "This realism is pitiless, violent, on a large scale, occasionally comical, with deep blacks, sulphurous yellows, bright reds. Its main object is to present men in their daily existence, to tell us of their work, to show us their defects and their passions. But all this is offered us pell-mell, in a way which cannot but surprise us, with outbursts of lyricism, punctuated with accents of grating irony, with nothing attentuated, soft-pedaled, or polished. It appears that one of the preoccupations of William Faulkner is to present us tragedies in the raw, without preparation, to use his characters somewhat as symbols and to give his landscape, smells, and lights the same importance as his characters, everything being blended and interwoven."[12]

Such a statement enlarges considerably Faulkner's figure. The publication of *Sartoris* in 1938 will allow us to take two more steps forward. "William Faulkner is a great novelist," states Edmond Jaloux in reviewing the novel, "and undoubtedly the most original postwar writer after Kafka and Virginia Woolf." While his technique may seem too disorderly to those who remain attached to the canons of classical art, "we cannot but feel dazzled by such vitality, by this overflowing power and the strangeness in this power." Jaloux uses

[12] *Europe,* September 18, 1934.

the words *magie poétique* and he brings out also in the very first sentence of his article the collective aspect of the Faulknerian creation. *"Sartoris,"* says he, "is not a character but a family, almost a human species."[13] To find a home for this *espèce humaine* and a few others, Faulkner, in following years, was to create the county of Yoknapatawpha, a map of which can be found on the last page of *Absalom, Absalom!* This "human comedy" aspect was emphasized later by R. N. Raimbault in his preface to *Treize histoires,* published in 1939.

Sartoris marks Jean-Paul Sartre's entrance in the field of Faulknerian exegesis. What strikes him in Faulkner's technique is what he calls his *déloyauté,* his art of dissimulation, his insistence upon remaining secret, his faith, "half-secret, half-dreamed, in the magical power of stories." Conjuration, bewitchment, and also solitude and silence. "Silence outside of us, silence inside of us, such is the impossible dream of a puritan stoicism."[14] From these silences Faulkner's novels draw their greatest power, and his most striking characters are those who cannot or will not express their thoughts. Already in 1931, James Burnham had stressed this point: "The most central intuition in Faulkner, that from which arise all the most deeply emotional situations, is a feeling toward inarticulateness. . . . I know no other writer whose work may in a very real sense be said to grow from the passionate awareness of inarticulateness."[15]

The following year *Le Bruit et la fureur* gave Sartre an opportunity to treat two of his favorite themes—Liberty and Time. He shows us Faulkner's heroes as prisoners of Time, out of which they try to disentangle themselves, but vainly because Time does not permit anyone to escape. Past remains and cannot be forgotten. Contrary to what happens in the case of Proust's time—a time lost but sooner or later recaptured—in

---

[13] *Les Nouvelles littéraires,* September 17, 1938.

[14] *La Nouvelle revue française,* L (February 1938), pp. 323–28; reprinted *Situations I,* pp. 7–13.

[15] "Trying to Say," *The Symposium: A Critical Review,* II (January 1931), pp. 51–59. This article is not mentioned in R. W. Daniel's bibliography.

Faulkner the past is never lost. It is always there. It is an obsession. Faulkner shows the events after their occurrence: "In *Le Bruit et la fureur* everything takes place backstage. Nothing happens, everything *has* happened. . . . One could compare Faulkner's vision with that of a man seated in an open car, looking at the receding landscape."[16]

So, at the time of the Second World War, the main aspects of Faulkner's genius had been, if not completely investigated, at least clearly indicated. After the Liberation, which marks the climax of the popularity of American novels, all the critics busied themselves studying Faulkner's works from the angle most appropriate to their personal temperament. Jean Pouillon, for instance, under the title, "Temps et destinée chez Faulkner," continued the investigations of Sartre.[17] Claude-Edmonde Magny also examines the Faulknerian conception of time, but she gives more attention to the mystical elements of Faulkner's novels, to their theological and mythical implications, and to their primitivism.[18] In a review of *Pylone* André Rousseaux comments on the subjective quality of Faulkner's realism and emphasizes the solitude which his characters unsuccessfully try to escape: "The drama of solitude is one of the grand themes of contemporary literature. I do not think that anyone has ever analyzed its desolation with a more refined cruelty than Faulkner." This is true particularly in the case of its most dreadful form: "the solitude of human acts which he observes as they try, desperately and vainly, to slip their effectiveness between the blind wheels of destiny."[19]

In the speech that he delivered at Stockholm, William Faulkner states what he considers to be the proper themes

[16] "A Propos de *Le Bruit et la fureur:* La Temporalité chez Faulkner," *La Nouvelle revue française,* LII (June 1939), pp. 1057–61, and LIII (July 1939), pp. 147–51; reprinted in *Situations I,* pp. 70–81.

[17] *Temps et roman* (Paris: Gallimard, 1946), pp. 238–60.

[18] "Faulkner ou l'inversion théologique," *L'Age du roman américain* (Paris: Editions du Seuil, 1948), pp. 196–243.

[19] *Le Littéraire,* October 19, 1946.

of the art of fiction: ". . . the old verities and the truths of the heart, the old universal truths lacking which any story is ephemeral and doomed—love and honor and pity and pride and compassion and sacrifice . . . the problems of the human heart in conflict with itself which alone can make good writing because only that is worth writing about, the agony and the sweat."[20] These themes have been for a long time the very essence of our greatest novels. This is undoubtedly one of the many reasons why France, for twenty years, has seen in William Faulkner one of the most remarkable analysts of the human heart, the man whom André Rousseaux has called *"le plus grand tragique de notre époque."*

[20] *William Faulkner's Speech of Acceptance upon the award of the Nobel Prize for Literature, delivered in Stockholm, on the tenth of December, nineteen hundred fifty* (limited ed.; New York: Random House, 1951).

ON TRANSLATING FAULKNER*

To the countless people who have on many occasions asked me how it is possible to translate Faulkner, I inevitably give the same answer: the problems which Faulkner presents are no different from those presented by all great novelists; and I add—a remark which sometimes occasions surprise—that if he is difficult to translate, he is, on the other hand, one of the authors whose works bear up best under translation. By that I mean that they lose of a minimum of their original quality.

The faithful reproduction of a text, which is naturally indispensable in a good translation, is not however the point on which the translator must concentrate his greatest efforts. What is most important to obtain is a translation which will give to the foreign reader the same impression that the original text gives to the reader in whose language it was written. An error in the interpretation of a question in detail, a mistake in a technical word, and even the voluntary substitution of one word for another (a procedure which is often necessary when it is a matter of names of birds, fish, or flowers) are only venial sins. On the other hand, to modify the general style of an author or,

* From *Princeton Alumni Weekly* (April 29, 1960), pp. 3–4. Reprinted by permission of the editors.

what is even worse, to substitute for it one's own style is the cardinal sin of inexperienced translators. A translator who would not make it possible for his readers to recognize immediately the style of Hemingway, let us say, or that of Thomas Wolfe, would be an execrable translator even if one could find no error in his text. When, in 1936, I undertook the translation of *The Sound and the Fury*, Faulkner was not unaware of the risk involved for his favorite novel. "I want to see this translation, indeed," he wrote to me on February 26, 1937, "because I feel that it will probably be a damned poor book, but it may be a damned good one (in French, I mean, of course) but in either case, particularly in the latter, it will be Coindreau and not Faulkner, just as the Rubáiyát which English speaking people know is a little more Fitzgerald [sic] than Khayyám. Have you any such feeling about it?" This feeling is known to every translator, above all at the beginning of his career, until he arrives at the point at which, like the chameleon, he adopts the color of the book he is translating without being aware of it.

The only means of avoiding the substitution of one's own style for that of the author is to respect scrupulously all of his stylistic habits. For example, the translator should not chop the author's longer sentences into small segments, nor inversely string together his shorter sentences to make long ones. The choice of vocabulary is of prime importance. To a style in which archaisms or poetic images are abundant should correspond a style of the same color in the language of the translator. Should the original author be obscure or difficult to follow, or should he impose upon his readers a constant effort, the translation must exact from its public the same labor and force its readers to surmount the same obstacles, thus refraining from rendering simple a text which is not so in the original language.

TRYING FOR OBSCURITY

This last point is one on which the translation of Faulkner presents the greatest difficulties for a French translator. It is more difficult to be obscure in French than in English. This phenomenon is due largely to the virtually complete absence in French of neuter pronouns and to grammatical rules which require that adjectives and participles agree in gender and number. I do not know what William Faulkner thinks of my translation of *The Sound and the Fury*, whether he finds in it more of Coindreau than of Faulkner, but I know that in spite of my constant efforts to preserve the obscurities of the text, the story in French is clearer than in English, a fact which causes me some regret. On the other hand, the long narrative sections of *Requiem for a Nun* can be reproduced in French without sacrificing their rhythm and movement, in spite of the syntax, with its complexity of structure, its cascades of subordinate clauses, its single and double parentheses, etc.

Ambiguity is one aspect of Faulknerian obscurity. The English language lends itself readily to multiple interpretations, an exceptional case in French. This was the problem faced by the translator of *The Unvanquished*. Is *unvanquished* in the masculine or the feminine, in the singular or the plural? The translator chose the masculine singular. In my opinion, this is an error. Had I translated this novel I would have titled it *Les Invaincues*, thus employing the feminine plural, and would have justified my choice by pointing to the many cases in which Faulkner uses this word in connection with those Southern ladies who have yet to accept defeat, and who ostentatiously leave the motion picture theaters when *Gone with the Wind* is presented. But the masculine plural would be equally acceptable.

LIGHT IN AUGUST

And I might bring up the old question of *Light in August*. The novel appeared in October, 1932. One could see on the jacket and on the title page great streaks of light, and everyone interpreted *light* as a noun. On March 12 of the following year there appeared in the column "Turns With a Bookworm," by Mrs. Isabel M. Paterson, in the Sunday book section of the *New*

York Herald Tribune, the following lines: "That reminds us, rumor says that Ben Wasson was particularly pleased with the title of Blair Niles's new novel, *Light Again,* because he also thought Faulkner's *Light in August* was a wonderful title. . . . Maybe it is, but evidently Ben does not understand what Mr. Faulkner's title signifies. . . . In fact, nobody seems to have even wondered what it means; so we will divulge the fact that it has no reference of illumination. . . . The 'light' means the opposite of heavy; and Ben may get a glimmer of the idea by searching through English history till he learns what Queen Elizabeth said when she heard that Mary Queen of Scots had produced an heir to the throne of Scotland."

This is to my knowledge the first mention of a possible ambiguity. I took it merely as a witticism typical of the style of Isabel Paterson, and when I undertook the translation of *Light in August* the following year, I called it *Lumière d'août.* Out of simple curiosity when I went to visit Faulkner in 1937, I called the matter to his attention. He seemed amused at the idea of this possible double interpretation, but he assured me that he meant nothing but the light of the month of August. However, the interpretation of *light* as an adjective has not yet been abandoned. In 1946 Malcolm Cowley put forth an idea which seems to agree with that of Mrs. Paterson, but which gives to *Light in August* a much less aristocratic origin. "In the Mississippi backwoods," he wrote, "it is sometimes said of a pregnant woman, but more often of a mare or a cow, that she will 'light' in August or September." In 1958, William Faulkner, in one of his class conferences at the University of Virginia, settled the matter once for all: *"Light in August,"* said he, "refers to the texture of the light in August in my country, in a spell of two or three cool days we call 'Blackberry Winter.' It's the light. I had never heard that business of after the cow drops the calf she's light in August."[1]

---

[1] *Faulkner in the University,* ed. Frederick L. Gwynn and Joseph L. Blotner (Charlottesville: University of Virginia Press, 1959), p. 265.

Such are some of the problems which the prose of William Faulkner poses for his translators. There are others. I have often been asked, "How can you translate dialect?" This is, in my opinion, a detail of slight importance. If the country people in Faulkner's work speak a Mississippi dialect, they speak above all as country people do, and nothing else matters. The same reasoning may be applied to Negroes. If Dilsey, the admirable "mammy" of the Compson family in *The Sound and the Fury,* retains our attention, it is not because of the color of her skin. What makes her a great figure of fiction is the nobility of her character, her qualities of devotion, abnegation, and endurance, all of them qualities which can be rendered in any language without detracting in the least from Dilsey's greatness. All men of my generation in France have known in the homes of their parents and their grandparents white counterparts of Dilsey. We know how they spoke and this is the only thing that concerns us.

My satisfaction was great when, upon reading the interviews at Nagano when Faulkner was in Japan, I came upon the following statement in answer to the question: "What part of the dialect did you use in your work?"

"I doubt if I ever used any dialect, except possibly the one that I speak myself. That is, the dialect is a good deal like something I said about style. The moment, the character, the rhythm of the speech, compels its own dialect. One moment the character can speak as a countryman, then when the need comes he will speak as a poet, but still in the phraseology of his background. I think to set out to write in dialect is as wasteful as to set out to write in style."

Any translator who knows how to write will find no difficulty in reproducing these "moments, characters, rhythms of speech," and if he knows his mother tongue well, he will know how to make a peasant or a poet speak convincingly. If he were to forget the principles so intelligently set forth by William Faulkner, he would run the risk of making a colored woman from Mississippi talk like a Negress from Martinique, Guadeloupe, or Haiti—an error similar to the one which Ernest Hemingway committed in *For Whom the Bell Tolls,* in which he used *thou* for the Spanish *tu,* and thus transformed a group of gypsies into a meeting of Quakers.

William Faulkner is a difficult author, and consequently one who gives to those who translate him the greatest of satisfactions, because a victory can be profoundly gratifying only if the adversary presents a real challenge. With the passing of the years and the evolution of Faulkner's art, the obscurity of his thought diminishes, but the complexity of his syntax increases. The syntax of *The Sound and the Fury,* for instance, would seem easy to the translator of the three stories which form the settings of the three acts of *Requiem for a Nun.* Such a translator would rarely have to wonder, "What does Faulkner mean here?" but he would constantly be lost in the entanglements of phrases which break off only to begin again two or three pages farther on, a phenomenon contrary to what has come to be considered good French prose. For that very reason, I know of no better professor of composition and style for Frenchmen, whose training has usually been directed along lines of extreme rigidity. Any translation will seem to be easy to the translator who has been formed under the tutelage of a novelist of this quality.

THE FAULKNER I KNEW*

If he were still among us, it surely would not occur to me to
reflect on the relationship that linked me, over a period of
thirty years, with William Faulkner. His role in my career as a
translator had become so important, he had become such a part
of my life that I no longer asked myself questions about him.
If I studied his work with my eyes as wide open as possible, I
accepted the man with my eyes closed and was no more concerned than he himself over the things that might be said
about him. But he is dead and already his image is becoming
blurred. Some who did not know him attempt to describe him
by using their imaginations. Television viewers were favored, I
understand, with comments on his oddities. The day after his
death one could see the words *imbecile* and *genius* coupled in
many a newspaper, not without perfidious intent. Let us not
discuss the errors that were spread everywhere. In a single article I learned first that he was born in Oxford. That is not true.

* From "Faulkner tel que je l'ai connu," *Preuves*, No. 144 (February
1963), pp. 9–14. The English translation, by James S. Patty, first appeared
in *Shenandoah*, XXVI, 2 (Winter 1965), pp. 27–35. Copyright ©
1965 by *Shenandoah*, and is reprinted by permission of the editors
and the translator. I have restored the somewhat polemical introductory paragraph, which was excised in the *Shenandoah* version.

In the early years of his career, it was said that Ripley was his birthplace, and for a long time I believed that assertion, attested to by the blurb for *As I Lay Dying* (1930). He was born in New Albany, Mississippi. I learned also that his wife had died the year before, whereas she actually closed his eyes and attended the funeral, bowed beneath a large black hat, as shown by a very fine photograph published in *Life* (July 20, 1962). I learned something even more astonishing. The author of that very instructive article, because he had not exchanged more than a few words with Faulkner while accompanying him on a battlefield, concluded that the novelist never talked with anyone. To strengthen the point, he wrote: "M. E. Coindreau, who translated Faulkner's first novels, scarcely got more than two sentences out of him in twenty years: 'How are you?' and 'So long.' "[1] Here we are no longer concerned with a factual error, something which can always be excused, but with a gratuitous assertion, a pure fabrication of a kind that gives the most false and unjust view of Faulkner's character. The same cordiality which he showed me at our first interview, in 1931 (for our relations lasted thirty years instead of twenty), prevailed also at the last dinner we had together, in 1959. Meanwhile, there had been various meetings, and I had always found him consistent with himself: not talkative, I admit, but always courteous, somewhat ceremonious, never giving me what I did not expect of him, but nevertheless surprising me at times by spontaneously telling me what I wanted to know but would not have dared to inquire about.

I am entirely aware that he did not show himself to everyone in the same light. There were several Faulkners. I will simply talk about the one I knew.

Having read, during the winter of 1931, not only *Sanctuary* (which came out in February) but also the five novels which preceded it and whose very titles I had not heard of until then, I wrote to Faulkner on March 23 to let him know of my

[1] Since I have not found the article in question, the phrasing in English **is mine.**

desire to be his translator, and I got in touch with his publisher, Harrison Smith. In October of the same year, Smith was kind enough to inform me that William Faulkner would be in New York at the very end of the month and would like to meet me over lunch. I would have forgotten the exact date of this meal if the dedication that Faulkner wrote that day on my copy of *As I Lay Dying* did not remind me of it: November 5, 1931. I returned to Princeton with the authorization to translate *As I Lay Dying* and any of the short stories I might like to choose from the volume which had come out two months earlier under the title *These Thirteen*. I knew that Raimbault and Delgove were working on a translation of *Sanctuary*. I had already prepared the ground by publishing, in the *Nouvelle revue française* for June, 1931, a short article designed to arouse the interest of French readers. Thus everything was ready for the offensive. Two stories, "Septembre ardent" and "Une Rose pour Emilie," appeared in early 1932, the former in the January *Nouvelle revue française,* the latter in the winter issue of *Commerce.* I had copies sent to Faulkner, and received the following letter from him, dated April 14, 1932:

Please accept these belated thanks for sending me La Nouvelle Revue in which was Septembre Ardent. I thought the translation excellent there, but the one of A Rose for Emily, in Commerce lost nothing at all, even of that which a writer perhaps alone feels in his story but never quite gets into the actual words. But principally I wish to thank you for your critique among the Lettres Etrangeres in a recent number of La Nouvelle Revue, which I received from a friend in Paris. I see now that I have a quite decided strain of puritanism (in its proper sense, of course; not our American one) regarding sex. I was not aware of it. But now, on casting back and rereading now and then or here and there of my own work, I can see it plainly. I have found it quite interesting.

Thank you again for your thoughtfulness in sending me the Revue.

The article in question was not as recent as he thought, since it dated from June, 1931. I had not mentioned it to him during our lunch in November, knowing that, even at that time, he had no interest in what people wrote about him. Five years went by during which I do not recall having seen him again. In August, 1933, I published "Il Etait une reine" ("There Was a Queen") (*N.R.F.*, August) and finished *Tandis que j'agonise* (*As I Lay Dying*), for which, back in 1932, Valery Larbaud had written a preface, but which went on sale only at the beginning of 1934, after the appearance of *Sanctuaire* with André Malraux's preface. Nineteen thirty-five was a productive year. I gave a story, "Soleil couchant," to the magazine *Europe* for its January issue, This prepared me to attack *The Sound and the Fury* and predestined me to translate *Requiem for a Nun,* since Nancy already appears in it, not working for Temple Drake but for the Compson family. Nineteen thirty-five is also the date of *Lumière d'août* (*Light in August*). I do not remember when I decided to undertake the translation of *The Sound and the Fury,* but a letter from William Faulkner, postmarked "Hollywood" and dated February 26, 1937, proves undeniably that I must have written to him right at the end of 1936, for in it he says:

This is mainly to ask your pardon for not answering your letter about 'Sound & Fury'. I probably stowed the letter away unopened, since I do not recall receiving one which I knew to be from you. I would not have been so discourteous otherwise.

Write me in care of the address below and I will give you any information you wish and I can about the book. After reading 'As I Lay Dying' in your translation, I am happy that you are considering undertaking S&F. I want to see this translation, indeed, because I feel that it will probably be a damned poor book, but it may be a damned good one (in French, I mean, of course) but in either case, particularly in the latter, it will be Coindreau and not Faulkner, just as the Rubáiyát which English speaking people know is a little more Fitzgerald [sic] than Khayyám. Have you any such feeling about it? Anyway, I wish you luck with it and I will be glad to draw up a chronology and genealogy and explanation, etc. if you need it, or anything else.

I will probably be in the East some time in this autumn. If I am, I hope we can have a meeting.

We met sooner. No doubt, when I thanked him for his kindness, I told him that I expected to spend the summer at Mills College, on San Francisco Bay, for on June 4, 1937, he wrote me:

> I have your letter. I will be here until August 15 and I will look forward to seeing you at any time you come to California at which time I will be glad to answer and try to explain any confusions in the book, though if you wish I will try to answer the enclosed questions by mail. I will await to hear from you again.

So I arrived at his house around June 20. He lived in Beverly Hills, in a pretty little California-Spanish style house at 129 Ledoux Boulevard. He would go to the studio in the morning, leaving me alone with his majestic Negro maid who had come with him from Oxford to keep house for him and to make sure that he lacked for nothing. She worshipped him and never ran out of things to say about him. How I regret that I did not take notes on everything she told me as she went about cooking and sweeping, her pipe in her teeth! In the evening, after dinner, I would bombard Faulkner with questions. This was still the period when self-styled serious critics claimed that, if one did not understand his books, the author himself did not know the meaning of what he wrote. Actually, he seemed to know *The Sound and the Fury* by heart, referring me to such and such a paragraph, to such and such a page, to find the key to some highly enigmatic obscurity. Only once was he unable to give me an answer. Unfortunately, I don't recall what sentence was involved. He read it, reread it, then began to laugh. "I have absolutely no idea of what I meant," he admitted. "You see, I usually write at night. I always keep my whiskey within reach; so many ideas that I can't remember in the morning pop into my head. As for the sentence in question, I must have had something in mind, but I can't tell you what." Similarly, the day I asked him why he had entitled one of his stories "Carcassonne," he was unable to give me a clear-cut answer.

"It's a vision," he said, "a poetic vision . . . a young man who sees a horse. . . ."

He drank. That was no secret to anybody. He did not try to hide it, nor did he boast of it like certain other writers of the "lost generation." He would go through tragic periods, but would emerge from his crises just as a strong swimmer succeeds in escaping from the undertow that carries him away. Personally, I never saw him give any embarrassing signs of drunkenness. While I was staying at his home, he drank constantly, but without seeming to be affected by it. On one occasion, however, he made me somewhat nervous. It was the day before I left; we had been to dinner at the home of a friend of his, a rich Englishman named Davenport, whose lush gardens overlooked Hollywood. There were a good many people present at this dinner, which was actually more a cocktail-picnic, and the evening went on till quite late. I had noticed Faulkner drinking constantly and felt rather uneasy thinking about the long ride in his high-powered convertible, over roads with hairpin curves. He got behind the steering wheel and set out at high speed. He did not go through one red light or scrape one curb, and got me home safe and sound without having said a word. I had not been in my room five minutes when he knocked at the door. He was holding in his hand a book and a few sheets of paper between two blue pages. "I would like you to take this volume as a souvenir of your visit," he said to me, "and take this story too. You expressed a desire to reread it. This way you will have the complete works of Ernest V. Trueblood." The book was a first edition of *Absalom, Absalom!* (which had come out in October, 1936), on which he had written his signature and the date, June 26, 1937. The pamphlet bound in blue paper was the typed copy of "The Afternoon of a Cow," which he had read aloud one evening, after a dinner at which he had assembled around his table two old friends from Oxford, Mr. Davenport, and myself. In the review *Fontaine* (June 1943), I have related the life and death of Ernest V. Trueblood, the nonexistent secre-

tary whom Faulkner had invented merely to have him write that
"in the manner of" which he later used in *The Hamlet*. Such is
the only testimony I can give as to William Faulkner's behavior
in a highly intoxicated state. That was twenty-five years ago. I
saw him several times afterwards in varied circumstances: at the
dinner Robert Haas held in his honor in New York, on the eve
of his departure for Stockholm; in Princeton, at the home of his
friend Saxe Commins; and in meetings with university students.
I never saw him other than sober, or at least apparently so. As
far as I am concerned, no unpleasant recollection stains his
memory.

After attaining fame, he raised ever higher the wall behind
which he sheltered (in that silence whose existence Dominique
Aury revealed in two wonderfully true and penetrating pages)
the dark secrets of Yoknapatawpha County and the ghosts of
Jefferson with whom he kept company. But his deeper nature
did not change, and if, on occasion, he rid himself of some pest
with a devastatingly laconic remark, he was also capable of sur-
rounding certain of his gestures with a surprising graciousness.
For example, in the first week of June, 1953, having stopped at
Princeton with Mrs. Faulkner while en route to Pine Manor,
the school where their daughter Jill was finishing her studies
(and where he had agreed to give a short speech for the grad-
uation ceremony) , he had his editor, Saxe Commins, at whose
house he was spending the night, phone me. He wanted, his
host told me, one of my translations of one of his books; any
one would do. The next morning I took him a copy of *Lumière
d'août,* and, intrigued by this odd request, I asked him for an
explanation. "It's for a lady at Pine Manor," he answered,
"who, my daughter wrote me, would like to have a signed copy
of one of my novels. Since she is in charge of the French courses
there, I thought that one of my books written in the language
she teaches would give her twice as much pleasure." Whether
the lady found out what was behind this gift which, no doubt,
she would have preferred to read in the original language, I

could not say; but, on the other hand, I am certain that, when he offered it to her, Faulkner said nothing to enlighten her, for he was extraordinarily reticent about his inner feelings. Taking someone into his confidence would have struck him as unseemly, and, judging others by himself, he would have feared to embarrass them.

Hence, when he signed his books—and he did so very rarely— he confined himself to the minimum. On my copy of *As I Lay Dying* he simply put: "With gratitude to M. Coindreau, the translator"; on *The Sound and the Fury* and on *Light in August,* my name, his signature, and the date. On *Absalom, Absalom!* he added the place, Beverly Hills. His dedications were equally concise. Once, however, he let his heart speak— the day he dedicated one of his most famous books, *Go Down, Moses,* to his family's Negro servant: "To Mammy, CAROLINE BARR, Mississippi (1840–1940), who was born in slavery and who gave to my family a fidelity without stint or calculation of recompense and to my childhood an immeasurable devotion and love." He had waited until the beloved centenarian had been dead for two years to pay her this touching tribute, for *Go Down, Moses* dates from 1942.

If he wanted to speak well of you, he preferred to do it when your back was turned. It has been reported to me several times that in the course of his talks with students at Princeton or at the University of Virginia, he mentioned my translations in terms which might have flattered my vanity. He never did it when he knew that I was in the room; and the two letters I have quoted above are the only written documents I could bring forward to attest his satisfaction. One evening, however, in the privacy of a dinner at Dorothy Commins' home—this was in 1959, and I never saw him again—he brought me around, by way of replying to a mildly eulogistic phrase, to expressing my ever present fear of not having done full justice to his works and of having betrayed him, involuntarily of course. He then became almost garrulous.

"You don't have to worry about that," he said to me. "As soon as my books are put on sale, they no longer belong to me. They belong to those who buy them. They can do as they please with them. I am no longer their owner."

"Still," I said, "Haven't you ever protested against Hollywood's infamous adaptations?"

"No. Why should I? First of all, I haven't been to see them, and, then, they too are free to use my books as they see fit. After a novelist has finished a book and given it to the public, there's only one thing left for him to do—start another one. The preceding one is no longer his."

This attitude, so rare among writers, can be easily explained (just as "the Faulkner mystery" can, assuming that there is a mystery) if one always keeps in mind the fact that Faulkner, beginning with the day he wrote *Sartoris,* no longer lived in our world. That is the meaning which must be given to the very true remark of Michel Mohrt: "He died with Bayard Sartoris, aboard a fighter plane, in the sky over France." Thereafter he only "appeared" among us. His true domain was the town of Jefferson and Yoknapatawpha County. For him, it was not Alceste's "desert"; rather it was Wonderland—a land of wonders often hideous and terrible—where the whiskey bottle played the role of Alice's mirror. For he drank far less to destroy himself than to create. With the odds and ends of reality offered by Oxford, Ripley, and the history of his family as a basis, he had begun to build his imaginary city and to people it with inhabitants. If he had been as stupid as certain people would have us believe, he would have made the Compsons and Sartorises paragons of all the virtues. But such is not the case. His "unvanquished ones" are just as vice-ridden as the Snopeses: "Faulkner [I borrow this quotation from Dominique Aury; I could not possibly improve on it] is no more merciful to his people than the Creator to the race of Cain and Abel. He holds them in his hand, turns them around, turns them back again without comment, puts them on display, and keeps silent."

It was in the silence of long nightly vigils that he cast the spells drunk from a liquid which, in Poe's time, would have been called "ignoble." This silence was not to be broken by anyone. Hence he avoided anyone who might have asked him troublesome questions or tried to sneak behind his back into that little kingdom of which he was the lord and master. I have often thought that he must have done violence to his own feelings to reveal to me, as he did in 1937, the origin of *The Sound and the Fury*, to explain to me its obscure points, and to confirm me in my idea that *Light in August* meant *Lumière d'août*, as I had translated the phrase in 1935, and not *légère en août*, as Isabel Paterson had suggested in 1933, long before Malcolm Cowley had set forth, in a different form, the same absurd opinion.

I repeat, Jefferson belonged to him and to him alone, and no monarch ever had such docile subjects. If he needed one of them, he would call him and restore him to life without worrying about whether what he was going to have him do was or was not compatible with the role that he had played in previous works. Sticklers for detail, armed with calendars and family trees, point out contradictions, chronological impossibilities, and odd reversals of the seasons in the chronicle of Yoknapatawpha. To these finicky people, Faulkner replied that his characters belonged to him, that he took them wherever and whenever he liked, heedless of other considerations. A creator is not bound to be a courthouse clerk as well.

But, however docile Jefferson might be, she found a way to take her revenge. She made her master her slave. She imposed attitudes, opinions, and ideas which transformed him into a citizen of Jefferson. The people, the animals, the buildings that he loved were part of the landscape of Yoknapatawpha. He was a great hunter, and his game was occasionally a bear, more often 'possum or raccoon, because that was what Major de Spain or Boon Hogganbeck might have hunted. Even if it had occurred to him to go off to the green hills of Africa in quest of more dangerous and more photogenic beasts, Jefferson would have forbidden him to go in for such safaris à la Tartarin. When he came into some money and bought what he called his "farm," what did he do but become the owner of an old house in Jefferson, with its white columns and tree-lined walk, the kind of house where Colonel Sartoris, Miss Rosa Coldfield, Miss Jenny, and perhaps even the perverse Miss Emily might have lived? A citizen of Jefferson does not build a Le Corbusier–style house for his abstract paintings, with swimming pool and garage doors that open at the mere sight of lighted headlights. That would give evidence not only of real foolishness, but of an unforgivable lack of taste. For Faulkner's readers, Jefferson is the ghost of Oxford; for William Faulkner, Oxford had ended up by becoming the ghost of Jefferson. Thus he was seen strolling around town with an absent-minded expression, lost in his visions, just as, in *Light in August,* Reverend Hightower, sitting at his window, listened to the sound of military fanfares and cavalry charges in a past of which he was the prisoner.

While our relations were always most cordial, they grew no closer during the thirty years that they lasted. The last time we met, it was just as if we were seeing each other for the first time. He was not one of those people who slap you on the back and call you by your first name five minutes after being introduced. He had not forgotten our long conversations of 1937, and I knew that, though he was not seeking me out, he did feel some pleasure at seeing me again. But there was nothing of the citizen of Jefferson about me. As familiar as his work was to me, what I knew of it was the printed volumes which had become the fare of readers, critics, and moviemakers—prodigal sons who had left their father's house—in other words, stories in which he had lost interest, as animals lose interest in their young, who are guarded and protected at their birth as jealously as Faulkner guarded and protected the creations of his genius before allowing them to leave Yoknapatawpha and go out into the world.

The gods gave him the death he would have wished for. He

had finished the Snopes trilogy. The chronicle of Jefferson was closed. The Compsons, the Sartorises, and the Sutpens had given way to the Varners and Snopeses, just as the Chickasaws of Ikkemotubbe, along with their queen Mohataha, had given way to the Sutpens, the Sartorises, and the Compsons. The cycle was complete. Only the final stroke was lacking, and this stroke was a burst of laughter, a piece of buffoonery—*The Reivers*. Then, the heart of the novelist, who for thirty-five years had suffered all the passions of his tortured characters, suddenly found itself out of work. It stopped beating. Faulkner could not die like Hemingway or Marilyn Monroe—the big, splashy leave-taking (an accident? suicide?). There are no question marks after Faulkner's death. The man who had never wanted people to talk about his life was granted an end which could not lend itself to any gossip. It was a beautiful, simple, clean death— exactly the kind he deserved.

ONE YEAR AFTER HIS DEATH

FAULKNER IS STILL MISJUDGED

IN THE UNITED STATES*

A year ago William Faulkner was brusquely carried off by a heart attack. At that time I was with my friend Michel Mohrt at the French summer school of Middlebury College in New England. We looked at each other in consternation. Around us several hundred students, men and women, young and old, seemed not even to suspect that on this day, July 6, not only their country but the entire world had just lost one of the greatest novelists of our time. I did hear several comments but they were in the style of Agnes: "The little kitten is dead."[1] All except one, which came from the lips of a gray-haired woman. "Faulkner?" she said. "But I thought he had been dead for ages. Didn't he write in the latter part of the nineteenth century?" She had been a teacher for a great many years. Poor students! During the weeks that followed, all the newspapers printed articles on Faulkner (some of them harshly critical, others full of insidious little comments slipped in between the usual condolences).

After all, a Nobel Prize winner could not be ignored. Europe, on the other hand, was touched more deeply. He had been one

* From *Arts,* July 10 and 23, 1963. Reprinted by permission of Gallimard. Translation by G.M.R.
[1] Agnes in Molière's *School for Wives.*

of ours long before his own country had deigned to pay attention to him. A good while ago he had overthrown all our habits of composition and style and had shown us the fragility of rules and laws which until then we had believed to be imperative. From then on it was difficult for young writers to write as if Faulkner had not existed. Sometimes they even went too far. In the extreme they plagiarized. In his own country he was ignored until he wrote *Sanctuary,* and immediately afterwards the official voices decreed that Faulkner was not an author of good breeding. Clearly he did nothing more than to put his morbid imagination in command of a style in which all the rules of grammar were violated as savagely as was Temple Drake in the woods. The public accepted this opinion which encouraged laziness. Nevertheless, lured on by the corncob, many bought the book, while remaining faithful to the great established names of the "lost generation": Dos Passos, Fitzgerald, and Hemingway. But there were some under twenty who were waiting only to grow a little older before they entered the lists. First came such subtle artists as the admirable Carson McCullers, William Goyen, and Eudora Welty; a little later came a group still younger, Truman Capote, Gore Vidal, and William Styron. For all of these, Faulkner was the master; but even though they admired him, they feared him. They were afraid of imitating him unconsciously, knowing that they could never equal, much less surpass him. When I asked Styron why, between *Lie Down in Darkness* (a fine novel, but very Faulknerian) and *Set This House on Fire,* he had remained silent for so long, having written only the short narrative, *The Long March,* he replied, "I wanted to free myself from Faulkner's influence before starting another full-scale book. *The Long March* was my disintoxication exercise." And he did not use this word in a pejorative sense, rather the contrary. The "intoxication" had been necessary for him, but it had lasted long enough. Today the generation of Carson McCullers and William

Goyen is approaching fifty; that of Styron and Capote is around forty. They are already elders.

The very young seem to have no fear of Faulkner, but have they read him? What can a body of work which scorns the present and considers the future only with repugnance offer to young novelists whose first desire is to become and to remain up to date? Some of them find the spray of the New Wave especially savory, and the anti-novel, in a country which shudders at the mere thought of not being in the vanguard in all things, offers delicious titillation to snobbery.

Faulkner had the wisdom not to heed the call of the external world. What his inner voices told him was interesting in quite a different way. He knew that the human heart is the same in all latitudes and in all epochs, and that the only works which can endure are those which attempt to analyze it, to plumb its mysteries, however terrifying they may be. He knew that we live surrounded by Oedipuses and Jocastas, by Phaedras and Hippolytuses, and that the family of our nearest neighbors is doubtless only slightly different from the house of Atreus. Such was the source of his own mythology. Naturally he had to situate it somewhere, above all in a place where time would have little power over it. To that end, like the happy children of earlier times spending their vacation with their grandparents, he rummaged around the attics of his ancestors, and there he discovered some marvelous things. Through the windows of the past he saw still virgin forests where bears and deer and panthers ran. He saw Mohataha, the old Indian queen, make her mark at the bottom of a document which took away her royal power, and then, wrapped in her purple robe, still proud beneath her parasol in the wagon escorted by her young warriors, leave for the West, without once looking back, toward the concentration camps hypocritically camouflaged by the name of "reservations." He saw trappers and mysterious adventurers following ephemeral dreams of grandeur. He also saw frightful crimes. To shelter these treasures which he knew to be fragile, he built himself a town, Jefferson, in Yoknapatawpha. He enclosed himself in it and spent his life there. No one could get into it, but from time to time he opened the doors and let a few of the inhabitants go out bearing messages from their creator about the agony "of the human heart in conflict with itself." He knew that he would have found nothing in the external world that he could not have found in his own country. The pleasures of the child taking five turns around the Jefferson Square on his wooden horse would have taught him as much about certain forms of human delight as the undoubtedly ecstatic, and legitimately so, joy of the astronaut who turns around our planet for five days. So why look out beyond the walls of the enchanted town?

VIRTUOUS AMERICA

But this is not the way to gain the favor of the public, especially in a country like the United States, where the people want to learn how to enjoy the present, where they believe in the magnificence of the future, but where they apply themselves with sadistic passion to the destruction of every vestige of the past. Old forests, old houses, old roads, and old bridges—all such things go into the garbage can. All that is necessary to ease the public conscience is to preserve old things in murals or in very faithful models placed in small-town museums or national parks. Thus there is no hindrance to progress. Americans do not in the least share the views of Maurice Barrès,[2] and the fact that Faulkner is deeply rooted in place and time is first among the things that the majority of his fellow citizens find wrong with him.

To justify their attitude, they regard him only as a regional novelist, without taking the trouble to find out whether beneath that envelope, which is in fact strongly regionalistic, there

---

[2] French novelist who stressed the importance of place and tradition in the lives of individuals and nations.

is something else hidden. For that matter, what is more Spanish than Cervantes, more French than Balzac, more Russian than Dostoevsky? And yet—

Second cause for complaint: one day after I had given a talk on Faulkner in Europe to a group of leisurely ladies in a small Connecticut town, one of my listeners admitted that she did not understand how anyone could admire literary works so contrary to morality and good manners. I asked her what she had read.

"I started *Absalom, Absalom!*" she said, "but I couldn't get very far. The story is just too horrible." I pointed out to her that, after all, the story, as the title indicates, scarcely differs from that of Absalom, Amnon, and their sister Tamar, just as one can find it in the Book of Kings.[3]

"You read your Bible, don't you?" I asked.

"Oh, yes I do!" she replied. "But it is not the same thing at all. You see, we're used to things like that in the Bible."

She had seen one point very clearly, that elderly lady, but her vision was very fragmentary. She should have added that Biblical personages—like the heroes of mythology—are not citizens of free America, not people who are virtuous by definition, and that one must have a very dismal soul to suppose that the murders and atrocities which one accepts in Holy Scripture without raising an eyebrow can take place in one of the states of the Union right under one's nose, so to speak. And yet, the audacity for which one frequently hears Faulkner reproached is not the underlying reason for the hostility which his work encounters. The public dislikes him even more (although they prefer not to admit it) for being a reserved and discreet writer, and even worse, for being a difficult writer. One needs only to read the novels that young American novelists are writing today in order to realize just how very proper, I would even say prudish, Faulkner was. To be sure, he was not afraid of any subject,

[3] Actually the Second Book of Samuel.

but ever since his earliest works he understood that if the novelist owes it to himself to say everything, he must also know how to say it. From the French Symbolists, who were the poets of his adolescence, he had come to know the power of the unexpressed. He became a virtuoso in the art of suggestion.

One gray hair on a pillow was all he needed to reach the limits of horror in "A Rose for Emily." But what would one do today with such artful subtleties? The average reader nowadays demands that the *i*'s be dotted for him. (But Faulkner not only does not dot them; rather, if he found some dotted accidentally he would remove the dots.) The young American writers, consequently, have a very easy task. They fill tipcarts full of garbage and dump it on your head. This method provides novels that are easily read and that demand no preparation whatever. The only vocabulary that the reader needs to know is the one he has acquired from reading the graffiti on the walls of public toilets. Demanding no more than the effort of turning the pages, and overfeeding the beast that drowses in the heart of each one of us, these novels often manage to remain for several weeks on the list of the best sellers. (Examples: *The Carpetbaggers,* by Harold Robbins or *Another Country,* by James Baldwin.)

Not that Faulkner never figured on that list. He achieved it with *A Fable,* his only mediocre, not to say bad, novel, but one which was reassuring because it did not take place in Jefferson and because, in the form of symbolic soldiers, Christ and his apostles appeared in it. It was thought then that Faulkner had abandoned Hell for Heaven, and in order to encourage him along that way, which was not his, the Pulitzer Prize was awarded him. He was given the prize a second time, posthumously, for *The Reivers,* because in that book the reader found old acquaintances and familiar places, notably the bawdyhouse in Memphis fifteen years before Popeye installed Temple Drake there. Moreover, it was a book without complexity, a good loud piece of buffoonery in which Faulkner even allows himself to tell a few dirty jokes. A burst of laughter before the eternal silence. That surely deserved a reward. So William Faulkner died guilty of quite a few sins against his fellow citizens. First of all, he insisted on living in a world which was not theirs. They were Snopeses; he was Sartoris. In the second place, he wrote books of disheartening difficulty; and, though seizing every opportunity to affirm his faith in man and in his possible greatness, he made no attempt to conceal his view that the human fauna he was able to observe in America as well as everywhere else were a pretty sorry lot, quite paltry and contemptible, whose company was worth much less than that of the animals he loved: mules, dogs, and horses, which he was able to describe magnificently. I think it was Guy Dumur who called him "the greatest animal painter of our time." Nothing could be more correct.

NOBLESSE OBLIGE

Finally—an unpardonable crime in a country where exhibitionism and social promiscuity are raised to the dignity of civic virtues—he coldly and sharply refused to participate in any kind of publicity or to allow any intrusion into his private life. He was the despair of journalists, of reporters, of all those who could have beaten the drums for his work but who, to him, represented one of the most intolerable aspects of our modern civilization. Nevertheless, born a gentleman and remaining a gentleman, he was aware that certain circumstances impose certain duties. He read French fluently, spoke it badly, and wrote it worse, but he had found in our language two words which pleased him and about which he never made any mistake —*noblesse oblige*. He liked to use them in his books, usually in italics. After he had received the Nobel Prize, he put them into practice himself. "The farmer who likes to tell stories," as he described himself in order to get away from troublesome people, eventually turned into a cultural ambassador of his country.

In 1955 he left for Japan on an official mission. He did not return with a book about his travels. That was not his genre. But he conversed with groups of students, and these conversations, which were tape-recorded, were made into a book, *Faulkner at Nagano* (1956). Later he was to do the same thing with the students at Princeton as well as at the University of Virginia, where his words were again recorded (*Faulkner in the University*, 1959). He lent himself graciously to these conversations and responded with patience and gentility to the most absurd questions. He certainly would have much preferred to be let alone, but *noblesse oblige*, and when one is a Sartoris one knows what these words mean.

Now he rests beneath a tree in the modest cemetery of the small town of Oxford, Mississippi. Under that earth which he loved so much and which he served so well, he no longer dreads intruders. Of course, his papers will be rifled and the locks of his drawers will be broken. Numerous studies are already under way in various countries of the world, including even his own, where he has a handful of very fervent admirers. It matters little to him now. He sleeps in his country of Yoknapatawpha, more indifferent than ever to praise, as well as to the *"noirs vols du Blasphème épars dans le futur."*[4]

---

[4] Literally the "dark flights of Blasphemy scattered in the future." From "Le Tombeau d'Edgar Poe," by Stéphane Mallarmé.

PART THREE

CONTEMPORARIES AND SUCCESSORS

PREFACE TO

*NOUS LES VIVANTS**

The place was New York, the time December, 1933. Erskine
Caldwell, who had finally decided to leave his Maine forests,
had asked me to accompany him that evening to the Masque
Theater, where for the first time he was going to see the three-
act play that Jack Kirkland had extracted from his novel
Tobacco Road. I can still see him dressed like a lumberjack,
taking his seat in the third row of the balcony. He had the air
of an overgrown, timid child, with his fair Viking's face and the
smell of the forest which still seemed to permeate him. The
premier of *Tobacco Road* had taken place four or five days
earlier (precisely, on Monday, December 5, 1933), and the
public did not yet know whether it ought to laugh or grow indignant over this slice of life which was being served, if I may
put it thus, with a hot sauce. Some very daring scenes, some
excessively raw oaths caused rather unpromising shudders to
run through the audience. "This play will not last a week,"
Erskine Caldwell said to me. It is now 1937 and *Tobacco Road*
is still running. It is a success without precedent in Broadway

* From Coindreau's preface to a collection of stories from Erskine
Caldwell's *We Are the Living* and *Kneel to the Rising Sun*, published
as *Nous les vivants*, trans. Ed. Michel-Tyl (Paris: Gallimard, 1938) ©
Editions Gallimard 1938. Translation by G.M.R.

history, and it has hallowed the fame of two actors, Henry Hull and James Barton, and the reputation of a novelist who has become one of the most popular of his generation, that is, of the writers who are around forty.

In the same year, 1933, the censoring of *God's Little Acre* had brought Erskine Caldwell's name to the attention of the general public, but only a few literary people knew that he had already published two long stories, *The Bastard* (1929) and *Poor Fool* (1930) ; a collection of short stories, *American Earth* (1931) ; and, in 1932, *Tobacco Road.* Today his work has increased by two volumes of short stories, *We Are the Living* (1933) and *Kneel to the Rising Sun* (1935) ; a novel, *Journeyman* (1935) ; and two journalistic books, *Some American People* (1935) and *You Have Seen Their Faces* (1937). In 1936 *The Sacrilege of Alan Kent* was brought out in a de luxe edition, with woodcuts by Ralph Frizzell; this was a reprinting of the last forty-six pages of *American Earth,* of which it formed the third part, "In the Native Land."

This strange account of a tormented adolescence contains in embryo all of Caldwell's work. Clearly autobiographical in nature, *The Sacrilege of Alan Kent* shows us a child with an exasperated sensibility who witnesses, from a very early age, the most atrocious accidents, deaths, and crimes. In the manner of picaresque heroes he evolves in a world of misery and brutality. He carries with him a primitive sensuality that is aroused by odors of the earth and of animals. "Here in this city the men bathed themselves every day and the women bathed three or four times, but none of them ever smelled as nice to me as the youngest colt or even the oldest horse."[1] And again: "I always liked to go down to the pasture early in the morning and smell the horses after they had been eating grass all night. Whenever I stood close to them and put my hands under their manes and closed my eyes, I wished I had been born a girl so

---

[1] *The Sacrilege of Alan Kent* (Portland, Maine: Falmouth Book House, 1936) , p. 47.

I could kiss them."[2] He carries with him also dreams of purity and of beauty which make him desire creatures who are sisters to nymphs and hamadryads, but from this idealism born of unappeased sensuality he derives only a feeling of incurable solitude. "And now I knew I would always be alone in the world." Such are the last words of his confession which links Erskine Caldwell with the great uneasy authors of Anglo-American literature today. One thinks of the D. H. Lawrence of *St. Mawr* and *Lady Chatterley's Lover*, of the Sherwood Anderson of *Horses and Men* and *Winesburg, Ohio*, and of William Faulkner, primitive poet and servitor of ancient myths.

As a matter of fact, in Caldwell's work as in Faulkner's, lyricism is pervasive, concealed more often than not but at times bursting forth freely. It is what gives novels like *God's Little Acre* and *Tobacco Road* such a special savor, and what relieves, in the eyes of the squeamish, the excessive boldness of certain pages. And in the two authors it is the same lyricism with profound roots that only psychoanalysis could reveal. All the powers of the earth perform mysterious, lascivious dances around man. But while Caldwell nourishes his joy and humor on such wanton powers, Faulkner is disquieted by them and seeks to flee. I will cite as an example only the theme of honeysuckle, an essentially aphrodisiac theme in the work of both authors. Erskine Caldwell writes:

Then I fell on my knees and cried with joy because she had been made as she was and that she had been named Florence because in the warm honeysuckle air that lay over my bed I felt her come and cuddle around me and the fragrance of the bloom made my heart race excitedly as her eagerness was. We both knew now why God had made her with such passion and me a man because I had the strength of a giant with her, but the soft magic of her arms and legs in love around me was the joy that I remember.[3]

---

[2] *Ibid.*, p. 30.
[3] *Ibid.*, p. 55.

There is nothing like this among Faulkner's heroes. In *The Sound and the Fury*, Quentin thinks:

> When it [the wisteria] bloomed in the spring and it rained the smell was everywhere you didnt notice it so much at other times but when it rained the smell began to come into the house at twilight either it would rain more at twilight or there was something in the light itself but it always smelled strongest then until I would lie in bed thinking when will it stop when will it stop. . . . Sometimes I could put myself to sleep saying that over and over until after the honeysuckle got all mixed up in it the whole thing came to symbolise night and unrest. . . .[4]

And further on:

> Then the honeysuckle got into it. As soon as I turned off the light and tried to go to sleep it would begin to come into the room in waves building and building up until I would have to pant to get any air at all out of it until I would have to get up and feel my way. . . .[5]

This exaltation of the joys of the flesh and this feeling that in love man becomes the equal of God explain why, whereas Faulkner's women are only morbid and corrupt instruments of sin, Caldwell's women are, on the contrary, "pretty wenches with fine rosy cheeks," as Rabelais would say. They develop like splendid animals among males whom they drive wild. And because God has knowingly made them desirable, they are accompanied by a climate of healthy lubricity in which all their intimate objects participate. Erskine Caldwell has been able to construct stories around fancy panties or a garter without inconveniencing his reader with the stale odors of smutty jokes. In his most lewd passages, he makes one think of babies who smile sweetly while displaying, in complete innocence, that which propriety orders to be hidden.

Caldwell affirms, moreover, that he never smiles and is aston-

---

[4] *The Sound and the Fury*, pp. 210–11.
[5] *Ibid.*, p. 215.

ished that critics speak of his comic verve. Humor is so natural with him that he is not always conscious of it. Not attempting to be funny, he is sometimes irresistible. His entirely personal style of comedy rests in large measure on the burlesque unawareness which he gives his characters. It is made also of incongruities which are not, however, devoid of logic, and of characterizations which border on caricature. It is sly humor for which the American model is to be found in Mark Twain. The French reader will think rather of Maupassant, for he is the one, among the storytellers of our country, to whom Caldwell comes closest. They favor the same kind of unadorned narrative, the same dry irony, the same latent pessimism. But in Caldwell this pessimism readily turns to sadism and atrocity. In the domain of horror and cruelty, the American easily triumphs over the Frenchman. Edgar Allan Poe and Ambrose Bierce make a weighty heredity, but their descendants do not seem the least bit afraid of it. Fundamentally romantic, beneath a toughness that is purely external, the young literature of America still has a taste for tombs, and quivers at the odor of blood and decay. In the realm of the macabre it has demonstrated an unlimited imagination, this literature which elsewhere is so unimaginative. Hence it possesses poets such as Robinson Jeffers, who would be difficult to conceive outside the United States. If Erskine Caldwell had written nothing but *Poor Fool,* he would already deserve first prize in the nightmare competition. A few of the pages which follow would confirm that award.

The stories in the present volume are taken from the two collections *We Are the Living* and *Kneel to the Rising Sun.* All aspects of Caldwell, it seems to me, are illustrated here: a pantheistic feeling for nature translated with the aid of symbols as old as the world but eternally beautiful, humor and lechery, cruelties that are sometimes intolerable. There is also social satire, though it is incidental, for only rarely in his fiction does Erskine Caldwell reveal that his heart is in the right place. But if each one of his stories has its individuality, all have at least one common characteristic which binds them together. It is a basic originality due to an intense savor of native earth which rises and displays itself over each page like a huge flag with stripes and a constellation of forty-eight stars.

PREFACE TO

*POOR FOOL**

If the French reader were not already familiar with Caldwell's best work, I would be careful not to present *Poor Fool* to him as an introduction to this writer's art. I have, in fact, no illusions about the imperfections of this small early work, and I know that it could alert the public against the man who dared to conceive its strange subject. But I know also how much we can derive from it regarding the mind of an author who is known, and rightly so, as the most original of his generation.

In the history of American literature, the years following the First World War will remain years of violence. It was the period when the young brutally rejected those of their elders whom they regarded as too timid. Under the aegis of Theodore Dreiser, of Sinclair Lewis, and of Sherwood Anderson, they practiced full-fledged naturalism or undertook explorations of the unconscious, toppling idols and disregarding taboos. They thought of nothing but violent action. Gangsters, boxers, and whores replaced the genteel characters of Edith Wharton and Willa Cather. Hemingway wrote his first and best stories. Joseph Moncure March published *The Set Up* and *The Wild*

* From *Un Pauvre Type,* by Erskine Caldwell (Paris: Gallimard, 1945) © Editions Gallimard 1948. Translation by G.M.R.

Party. Erskine Caldwell got his hand in with *The Bastard* (1929) and *Poor Fool* (1930).

The first of these two narratives is distinctly inferior in quality. After a series of adventures as bestial as they are monotonous, Gene Morgan, son of a prostitute and an unknown father, finally goes to live with Myra Morgan (the same name— a half-sister perhaps?). A baby is born of this union, a hideous little monster with a hairy face. One evening Gene, pretending to take the baby out for some air, throws him into the river and then leaves, after a last glance at the window where the silhouette of Myra is visible as she anxiously awaits the return of the man and her son. There is nothing fanciful to brighten this grim story, which at times makes one apprehensive of discovering that the whole thing is a kind of provocation inspired by the desire to find out, through the accumulation of gratuitous horrors, how far an author can go before a reader revolts. Erskine Caldwell is not yet himself in *The Bastard.*

He is, on the other hand, completely himself in *Poor Fool.* When I asked him what had impelled him to write such a disconcertingly macabre story, he replied:

> I wanted to use the methods of realistic writing on a purely imaginary subject. When I was working on *The Bastard,* I was careful never to get away from the real, or at least the possible. More than anything else I wanted realism with verisimilitude. *Poor Fool,* on the other hand, belongs to the literature of dreams. It is something like those diabolical dreams that come out of opium, except for the fact that I have never used opium. I simply let my imagination run free, without barriers or restraints. Nevertheless, I tried all along the way to make my story ring true, and I believe that if it has any interest, the reason is the contrast between the madness of the subject and a style that is cold, concise, and perfectly reasonable in its strict objectivity.[1]

It is certainly true that this little nightmare derives part of its value from that contrast. But only part. *Poor Fool* is more

---

[1] Since there is no record of this conversation, the phrasing in English is not Caldwell's but mine, translated directly from Coindreau's version in French.

than a bad dream. It is the seed from which the true Caldwell will soon be born and, consequently, the thread of Ariadne which will eliminate the errors that are always possible in the interpretation of *God's Little Acre,* of *Tobacco Road,* and of the stories in *Nous les vivants.*[2] *Poor Fool* contains everything that makes up the fundamental originality of Mr. Caldwell: his taste for horror and cruelty, his very special way of regarding sexual matters, and that deadpan impassibility to which he owes his finest successes. Already we find the tragicomic marionettes which reveal him as a master of caricature: Mrs. Boxx and Jackie, whose naughty games prefigure the frolics of Dude and Sister Bessie (*Tobacco Road*), and the more cruel doings of Pluto and Darling Jill (*God's Little Acre*); and the alarming Mr. Boxx, a familiar of the kingdom of the dead, thanks to whom we understand why, in *Tobacco Road,* Ada Lester insists on being buried in a pretty, stylish dress. But it is especially the "poor fool," Blondy Niles, who should be set beside all the "poor fools," all the abulics that populate Caldwell's novels. In a very interesting study of *God's Little Acre* Lawrence S. Kubie insists that Caldwell is the painter of impotence and sterility. His male characters, even those who boast of their virility, never succeed in escaping entirely from their childhood. Against them are their mothers, who never appear in a normal light. "As the figures of women become clearer," writes Mr. Kubie, "the maternal role is distorted more and more towards perversion and prostitution." In Caldwell's works "there are good mothers who are dead, good mothers who suffer, bad mothers who hoard their sustenance and will not share, mothers who breed and transmit disease, erotic mothers whose bodies exist to nurse men, and women who exist only to destroy."[3] This comment sheds light on the ignoble Mrs. Boxx, the mon-

[2] For details about this collection of stories from *We Are the Living* and *Kneel to the Rising Sun,* see "Preface to *Nous les vivants*" in this volume.

[3] "*God's Little Acre:* An Analysis," *Saturday Review of Literature,* XI, No. 19 (November 24, 1934), p. 306.

strous mother, the source of destruction who turns all the "poor fools" into her slave-sons. *Poor Fool* is a chromo illustration of the Oedipus complex and of the castration complex. "I want to, but I can't get away," Blondy groans, in the grip of the terrible Genetrix. And the liberation which Dorothy brings him comes only as a prelude to death. Because *Poor Fool* is, by the author's own avowal, a novelized dream, one could not study it completely except by using Freudian methods. Psychiatrists will be grateful to Erskine Caldwell for having offered them a naturally savory dish that, for good measure, he has seasoned with a pinch of sadism and necrophilia.

There is, then, much more than one might believe in this narrative which is at once violent, horrible and grotesque, awkwardly executed, and slowed by the repetition and the monotony of a style whose rough staccato I have willingly respected. It was because of the profound resonances in this work that I developed an interest in presenting it to the French public.

I present it also for bibliographical reasons. *Poor Fool,* like *The Bastard,* has been published only in a limited edition.[4] Today it is an extremely rare work. Hence the present version has the interest of a first edition not only in Europe but for most American readers as well.

[4] *The Bastard* (New York: Heron Press, 1929), illustrated by Ty Mahon, was published in an edition of eleven hundred copies. *Poor Fool* (New York: Rariora Press, 1930), illustrated by Alexander Couard, was limited to one thousand copies. M.E.C.

PREFACE TO

*OTHER VOICES, OTHER ROOMS**

The years slip by and already we are beginning to glimpse the
main feature of what will be the face of the young American
literature in this postwar period. It is a serious face, coarse in
a rather common way, simple and with neither false nor genuine ornaments, and not at all like the face modeled by the
war of 1914. In those days one could rightly speak of a "lost
generation." The war had taught the members of that generation only to have doubts about a past of which they had been
the tragic conclusion. The young authors of 1920, after they
understood that they had been deceived, were angry with their
country, which they accused of glorifying false gods, of despis-
ing spiritual values, of ignorance, and of unconscious puerility.
To emphasize their point they went into exile. The marvels of
Montparnasse took the place of the lost illusions. They began
to write about new subjects with new techniques. They set out
to attack taboos and old restraints. They purged their hearts
of accumulated complaints of long standing, and then, girded
with the aureole that surrounds bad boys, they returned home
to enjoy the sometimes exaggerated homage of a public that
was partial to works smacking of wickedness.

* From *Les Domaines hantés*, by Truman Capote (Paris: Gallimard,
1949) © Editions Gallimard 1949. Translation by G.M.R.

Those who expected the writers of 1940 to behave like those of 1920 forgot that in order to be lost it is necessary first to find oneself. But the young writers of today have had neither the leisure nor the possibility to do that. Born in a time of financial disorder, brought up with the specter of a new war as their companion, they accepted without astonishment the catastrophe that arrived in celebration of their twentieth birthdays. Military operations, in which they participated much longer and more dangerously than had their elders, took them into a Europe which offered nothing to satisfy the desire for escape and the dream of paradise. They were not yet cynical—of all the virtues, cynicism is the one that the young American is least likely to acquire—but they were more mature than the "lost generation." Neurasthenia is not at the bottom of their revolt, and their despair is not that of a child whose pretty toys have been taken away from him. Instead of morose pleasure they choose defiance. They have not known order, and chaos interests them more than it frightens them. Their basic growth took place amid problems that are far from being solved. They are seeking less to flee than to understand and to organize. This fact explains their close contact with events. American literature is, consequently, more immediate than ever. To the jolts and starts of everyday life, each young American who can hold a pen responds with what he calls a novel, usually a thesis novel. Precious documents in the history of manners and even of ideas, these works suffer from a lack of incubation, from a hasty birth. Excellent reporting, these books have the spontaneity of a reflex but they belong to literature only by pretense, for a good journalist does not make a good novelist. However sharp a photograph may be, however close to current reality its subject may be, it will never be worth as much as a canvas that comes from the creative brush after a long gestation.

That is why *Other Voices, Other Rooms* stands apart from the general fictional produce of very recent years like an exotic flower among the modest flowers of the field. In it there is no question of war, nor of ideologies in conflict, nor of race prejudice, nor of social claims. The young man known to everyone by the name he adopted, Truman Capote, opens other rooms for us, and the voices he causes us to hear are at once more harmonious, more vibrant, and infinitely more moving than the clamor of GI's and of the advocates of all the freedoms and all the equalities. I hasten to say that this interpretation of the title does not at all correspond to the first intention of the author; but chance, wishing the title to have a double meaning, has placed the work in a period where it is clearly an exception.

When *Other Voices, Other Rooms* made its appearance in 1948, Truman Capote was not unknown. In 1946 a short story, "Miriam," published the year before in *Mademoiselle,* had won the O. Henry Prize; and the collection of the best American short stories of 1947 had included "The Headless Hawk." Magazine readers had seen in May, 1945, "My Side of the Matter" in *Story;* in October, 1947, "A Tree of Night" in *Harper's Bazaar;* and in August of the same year "Shut a Final Door" in the *Atlantic Monthly.* Hence it was already known that he avoided the worn trails, that he had taken possession of a clouded world, full of mystery, where the living had the form of ghosts and ghosts the form of the living. The writer of such disturbing stories could only be a legendary person. *Other Voices, Other Rooms* had hardly appeared in the bookstores when public rumor fabricated a biography for the author that was worthy of his stories. One lends only to the rich. But in the case of Truman Capote destiny proved to be exceptionally generous. The first years of his childhood, disturbed by the divorce of his parents, were passed at Placquemine, a plantation about sixty miles from New Orleans, the city where he was born (September 30, 1924). On that estate lived three of his aunts, and one of them, whose room he shared, kept him awake until late at night telling him strange stories of the region: real and imaginary crimes, folklore, superstitions. The child stored these nightmares away without suspecting that one day he would have to exorcise them by turning them over to printers. Such, until he was more than eleven years old, was his only vision of the world. He told his teachers and schoolmates about it as soon as he was sent to school. "That child is crazy," his astounded interlocutors said to the principal. "We can't keep him here." And little Truman was sent away. The same thing happened to him several times until one day in Greenwich, Connecticut, his English teacher, Catherine B. Wood, gave that craziness its true name. In the little newspaper of her school she has preserved the first stories of her pupil, for whom writing was already the best form of recreation. He stayed away from the great colleges, thinking, not without reason, that life would teach him more. From the Pacific to the Atlantic he was seen in all the states—small, stocky, with his fringe of blond hair and his eyes that gleam enigmatically behind large horn-rimmed glasses. He worked at some amazing trades and knew some amazing people. Under the name of "Old Captain Truman," he danced on one of the pleasure boats that travel up and down the Mississippi. He learned to paint flowers on glass, making them seem more mysterious by inserting filigrees of spider web between the panes. In New Orleans he became closely associated with Mrs. Acey Jones, who in earlier times would have been called a witch but who is satisfied to tell fortunes. He speaks of her as of a supernatural being, and his confidence in her is unlimited. Very sociable, he makes friends everywhere, and he is as much at ease in a dubious bar in some disreputable quarter as at the sumptuous Hollywood dwelling of his friend Charlie Chaplin. Like all his compatriots he has remained nomadic. He catches an airplane the way others catch a streetcar. You think he is in Europe and he sends you a card from Haiti or Cuba. But he prefers to live in New Orleans or in New York, in his small apartment or in the much larger one of Mr. Capote, his stepfather. He gets up at noon, sleeps after dinner until around midnight, and then begins writing. At dawn he returns to bed. In contrast to the young writers of his generation who pretend to read nothing (for fear, they assure us, of losing their originality), he reads at any hour of the day. Among his favorite writers are Flaubert, Henry James, Proust, Virginia Woolf, and Katherine Anne Porter. Closer at home he likes Carson McCullers and Tennessee Williams. He detests the "tough school" of novelists and fears, although he profoundly admires, William Faulkner. "One could be influenced by him without realizing it," he says. "That's why he is dangerous."

Last February all his short stories were published in a volume entitled *A Tree of Night*. To form a precise idea of his art it is indispensable to set these stories beside *Other Voices, Other Rooms*. The dominant impression they leave upon first reading is one of unreality. Enigmatic characters, driven by forces they do not understand, wander in worlds filled with voices, appeals, and signs. Most of them have some strange deformity: Miss Amy's crippled hand, Zoo's giraffe neck, or the club foot of Walter's companion ("Shut a Final Door"). Ambiguity is a constant factor. How old are they? What sex are they? From the lips of children come the disabused words of fully experienced persons. Little girls with white hair play at being ladies, and the adults have many childish traits. Randolph remains for Miss Amy the adolescent whose tragic life has never succeeded in transforming him into a man. The sex of these ageless creatures is also indefinable. There are Idabel the tomboy, Joel, who is too frail and too pretty, and Randolph, who asks himself, "Whatever became of me?" Women dress as men (Idabel, D. J. in "The Headless Hawk") and Randolph, in the semi-darkness of his closed room, puts on the gowns of a marquise. When an antithesis does not go so far as to take on a concrete form, it manifests itself in visions. The handsome Vincent ("The Headless Hawk") sees himself beneath the lineaments of a horrible old man with dyed hair, powdered cheeks, and Kewpie-doll lips, who fastens on his back like a frightful spider. All of them, whether they live in New York or in the gardens of Louisiana, are the landlords of haunted domains, of which they themselves are the most terrible parts. Their tormentors are not born of the air in the calyxes of flowers like sylphs; rather, like vapors ascending from swamps, they rise from the recesses of the unconscious, from the most secret box in Randolph's Chinese chest. Consequently the deformities with which they afflict their victims, far from making the victims unacceptable, increase their density and their verisimilitude, and one arrives at this conclusion which, at first glance, could seem paradoxical: that these quasi-monstrous beings are more real, more true, and infinitely closer to us than the soldiers in the manifold war novels who are condemned, by their photographers, never to have more than the two dimensions of decals. The Capote characters possess the hallucinatory qualities of figures in dreams, and for them, as for their author, dreams are the only reality, the world around us being only illusion and vain appearance. To know themselves they make use of mirrors or of some portrait, for art is a means to knowledge: "Always for me," Randolph explains, "there is the problem of distortion, and I never paint so much what I see as what I think: for example, some years ago, this was in Berlin, I drew a boy not much older than yourself, and yet in my picture he looked more aged than Jesus Fever, and whereas in reality his eyes were childhood blue, the eyes I saw were bleary and lost. And what I saw was indeed the truth. . . ."[1] Because Joel and Zoo have a common faculty for living in kingdoms of fantasy, would it be correct to accuse them of lying? When Joel, for the benefit of the Negress, falsely described the death of his mother in the Canadian snow, his tale "seemed more real than Missouri and her long neck, or Miss Amy, or the shadowy kitchen."[2]

If I have cited this dream of snow from among the abundant dreams in *Other Voices, Other Rooms,* the reason is that the

[1] *Other Voices, Other Rooms* (New York: Random House, 1948), p. 136.
[2] *Ibid.,* p. 59.

theme of snow is a constant leitmotiv in the work of Truman
Capote. One hears this theme many times in *Other Voices, Other
Rooms,* and although none of the stories that make up *A Tree
of Night* is entirely devoted to snow (as is the case with a little
masterpiece by Conrad Aiken, "Silent Snow, Secret Snow"), at
least there is snow to be found in most of them. To uncover the
reason, it would be necessary to enter the domain of psychoanalysis. I will say only that this detail—one could cite a
number of others—would suffice to make this young man named
Truman Capote a brother of the great anxiety-ridden men
of literature: Baudelaire, Mallarmé, and especially Edgar Allan
Poe (one should recall in particular the final pages of *The
Narrative of Arthur Gordon Pym*). As a remedy for anxiety
the snow brings its purity, its transformation of a hostile world
whose harsh ugliness and too sharp edges it softens. But especially, with its immaculate blankets, dispensers of silence, it
offers to the wounded solitary person the asylum which he
seeks. Alone—all the characters of Truman Capote are terribly
alone. "Are the dead as lonesome as the living?" asks Miss
Wisteria.[3] Their solitude results from their ambiguous nature,
which condemns them to instability, to the misunderstanding
of others, and—what is worse—to their own misunderstanding. Each one of them must live with an incomprehensible
double whom he cannot reject and with whom no understanding is possible. This is the meaning of the last lines of "The
Headless Hawk," in which D. J. ends by uniting with Vincent
while a torrential rain puts a glass curtain between them that
will separate them always.

From such inexorable solitude is born a morbid desire for
affection ("God, let me be loved," Joel prays. "I love you," he
says to Zoo, "because you've got to love me because you've got
to."[4]) and a touching need to be protected, consoled, reassured:
"Tell me what I want to hear," Randolph says to Joel, after

[3] *Ibid.,* p. 205.
[4] *Ibid.,* pp. 74, 117.

his pathetic confession. And Joel answers: "Everything is going to be all right."[5] Unfortunately, nothing turns out all right. In order to find some reason for living, these poor lost creatures beguile themselves by creating an illusion. For Zoo it is Washington, D.C., for Miss Wisteria a little boy who will not "grow tall," and for Randolph an almanac which lists all the cities of the world. Having been raped and tortured, without having seen the capital, Missouri returns to the Landing; Miss Wisteria, searching for Joel, probes in vain with her flashlight in the abandoned house; and Randolph never receives a reply to his daily letters.

The work of Truman Capote is marked by despair, and the sadness in it is all the more poignant because, at times, a roguish smile betrays the extreme youthfulness of the writing. Childhood is not so far away from Capote that he cannot remember its gaiety and its enchantments. But life, and the world with its malice, have shown him what is hidden behind the masks. The mixture of great wisdom and candid simplicity is one of the principal charms of Truman Capote's fiction. The style is another. There again he differs from the young people of 1940 for whom writing is less an art than a duty of good citizenship. In Capote one notes a constant concern for the artistic effect. His prose is beautiful because of its richness, because of the masterly choice of words which heighten the scale of colors, the sensuality of odors, the variety of sounds. It is a musical prose, impregnated with "correspondences," and it changes according to the subject. Each of the short stories has its own rhythm, and in *Other Voices, Other Rooms* the characters use tones and tempos which, more than the words they pronounce, shed light on their inner nature. Zoo's hymn-singing is answered by Miss Amy's complaints; Idabel's brusk staccato by the finical rubato of Florabel and Miss Wisteria. Randolph expresses himself in a style as rococo as the furniture in his room. Careful to

[5] *Ibid.,* p. 154.

bring out all the harmonies, the author directs his instruments like a meticulous, accomplished conductor. Consequently there have been critics who complained that the book was over-written. For if the success of *Other Voices, Other Rooms* was explosive (the ten thousand copies of the first edition disappeared in a few weeks), one must not think that the applause was unanimous. The partisans of socially committed literature found that Capote showed a sacrilegious indifference concerning the problems of the day. Some critics spoke also of morbidity, of sickly complaisance. That was the reverse of a medal whose obverse was a dithyramb sometimes completely out of proportion. The golden mean seems to me to be represented by John W. Aldridge, who in the *Saturday Review of Literature* writes very intelligently, although with too much prudence, as follows:

> It may be that *Other Voices, Other Rooms* will prove to be the most interesting stylistic departure to be made by a member of the younger literary generation. It may also be that Capote will prove to be the best thing that has happened to our literature since Hemingway and the most powerful antidote since Faulkner to the tradition of numbness and understatement which Hemingway introduced. But what he has given us so far is an exquisitely cut emerald, an expensive ornamental device. We may admire it, for it is indeed admirable, but we cannot identify the shadowy forms it reflects nor ascertain its true value or usefulness.[6]

Truman Capote is putting the final touches to a second novel, which he had thought of calling "Monday's Folly." He has changed his mind and abandoned this title. That is a usual event with him. Will it be a new "emerald" as prettily cut and with as pure a luster as the one he has recently offered us? Not being Mrs. Acey Jones, I would not dare to say, but I put faith in the author and envisage his future with the most complete confidence.

[6] "America's Young Novelists," *Saturday Review of Literature*, February 12, 1949, p. 42.

PREFACE TO

*THE HOUSE OF BREATH**

So long as the "lost generation" still shows a productivity that, though certainly diminished, is in no sense negligible, some undoubtedly will think it imprudent to oppose it henceforth with the constellation of young authors who each day make its wrinkles and white hairs stand out more sharply. The oldest of these young writers have barely passed thirty. Their baggage is still light, and prudence would undoubtedly command us to wait and see what the future holds for them. We can reply that if they do as their elders did, they will change very little. Thomas Wolfe died without making peace with a world that was too complex for his eyes of a childish giant, and Ernest Hemingway is still straining, with no more success than before, to kill great wild beasts and to catch huge fish. However, those who began their careers between the two wars had a longer way to go than the new novelists. Having begun as adolescents, most of them remained adolescent. Why should one expect a more rapid and radical evolution of a new group of writers whose maturity is already such that, compared to their predecessors, they look like old men. Apparently born disillusioned, or rather gifted with tragic insight, they have grown up without

* From *La Maison d'haleine,* by William Goyen (Paris: Gallimard, 1954) © Editions Gallimard 1954. Translation by G.M.R.

experiencing the dazzlement of youth. For them, *"le vert paradis des amours enfantines"*[1] has never been lighted except by the flames of hell. Even those who had not read Gide knew that man is a labyrinth and that to triumph over the Minotaur that sleeps within, one needs more than rodomontade and the skills of a Boy Scout. One must go courageously all the way to the depths of the lair, seize the beast, and dominate it by forcing it out into the full light of day. And that cannot take place without pain. The young American writers do not flee from their demons. They hunt them out and defy them, and do it even with a kind self-satisfaction. To be sure, the theme of escape remains a constant in their works, but it is escape with the hope of self-discovery, of self-knowledge, and no longer, as was the case with their elders, with the aim of avoiding oneself. It goes without saying that these few remarks apply only to the truly creative young artists, such as Carson McCullers, William Goyen, Gore Vidal, Truman Capote, and William Styron, to mention only the most important ones. What has been said is totally unrelated to a whole superficial literature (war stories, or novelized and usually tendentious exposés of social problems), which, written in the hard-hitting manner of twenty years ago, has more to do with reporting than with original creation and has added nothing to what we already possessed.

Monsters inhabit the literature of these young writers, and solitude is overwhelming in it. Isolated in a hostile world because of their physical or psychological deformities, the characters flounder like unfortunate animals caught in a trap. If they expect to be liberated, it is not through the obliteration of the senses or of thought, but rather the contrary. They are not naïve enough to believe, as ostriches do, that by hiding their heads in the sand they eliminate the danger. Ill-adapted to the present, they turn toward the past; for only an extensive knowledge of the past will permit them to choose the one route

---

[1] A line from Baudelaire's "Moesta et Errabunda."

among those of the future which, from the day of their birth, the gods have desired them to follow. Solitude is certainly not a new theme in American literature. The best representatives of the "lost generation" were familiar with it. They took it into bars with the hope of drowning it, or they fired on it with a revolver in order to frighten it. Sometimes they sent it out to tour the world. One should recall the melancholy heroes of John Dos Passos, poor cousins of Barnabooth, who carry their empty suitcases through five continents. Our youthful authors reserve their characters for voyages of a more painful kind, voyages not on the surface but in depth. Barrésians without knowing it, they root their characters in the earth which witnessed their birth and invite them to seek there for the answer to the questions that trouble them.

All indications are that, for these newcomers, works in the style of Hemingway no longer have any kind of value except historical. They find neither light nor comfort in such writing. Even less would they find encouragement there. On the other hand, they all bow before William Faulkner, whose descents into hell are at once an inspiration and a danger to them. They see in him the master who has been able to travel the road that Hawthorne had indicated (but with what caution and what reticence!), the road which, later, Sherwood Anderson bravely undertook to follow, and which henceforth is open to them. They are grateful to Faulkner for having written that the true novelist must have only one aim—the study of "the human heart in conflict with itself." They do not pretend to equal him and do not allow themselves to imitate him (at least consciously). Each one dons his own costume. Truman Capote drapes himself in the graces of childhood and dives into the abysses prettily dressed in delicate material which is enhanced as needed by a lace collar or a bow. Gore Vidal prefers a uniform, a business suit, or sportswear; and on occasion, knight's armor. As for William Goyen, it is in the guise of an Aegipan that I see him wandering around in Eastern Texas where he was born in 1918.[2] There he finds voluptuous and fruitful rivers in which to renew his fervor, and *"forêts de symboles"* that welcome the restless seekers of knowledge. Appropriating each one of Gérard de Nerval's *vers dorés*,[3] he casts no doubt on the idea that everything is sentient, that a *"mystère d'amour dans le métal repose"* and that to *"la matière même un verbe est attaché."* One breath is enough for the miracle to take place. Breath is the only instrument of this conjuration. Let it be exhaled and things become animated and in their turn breathe their words to us. Then the messages multiply, carried by the winds or upon the wings of birds. They spring up from the depths of cellars, from the sonorous darkness of wells; and the deep beds of streams teach disturbing lessons. Cries which were thought to be forever silenced, the voices of beloved persons long since dead, resound anew; for in this "Temple" which is Nature, every being's double is hiding, the ghosts whose manifestation awaits only the creative breath and the invitation of the senses. Then a magical universe takes the place of our world, a universe which, for William Goyen the poet, is the only one where man can hope to grasp the reality of all things and of himself. In the preceding lines I have intentionally multiplied the references to the great themes of our Symbolists, for *The House of Breath* is above all a poem. Goyen has used as an epigraph Rimbaud's line, *"Je est un autre."* I would have preferred the following line spoken by Mallarmé's Faun: *"Oh, Nymphes, regonflons des souvenirs divers."* Indeed, as Katherine Anne Porter has remarked, *The House of Breath* is "a sustained evocation of the past, a long search for place and identity, and the meaning of an intense personal experience; an attempt to cleanse the heart of its mysterious burden of guilt, to build with words, a breath-made

[2] Hence he belongs exactly to the generation of Carson McCullers (born in 1917), the prodigy of 1940, and ever since the admirable interpreter of the solitude of the heart. M.E.C.

[3] "Golden Verses," the famous poem pointing toward French Symbolism.

substance, a bridge over the gulf between two disassociated experiences."[4] In other words, it is at once a manual of fervor and a search for authenticity. When the wind brings Malley the words of her son Berryben, here is what she hears: "Of all the evils you taught and tried to teach me, the *only* evil is that we cut ourselves off from any force that wants to flow into us and use us like a turbine; or that when that force finds us we hold ourselves still, blind and deafen ourselves to it. The finding of that force, the awareness of it, quivering in us, trying to turn us so that we may generate, and the attempt to use it is to make oneself real. The substitution of any other force is a mechanical turning and is false; is evil."[5]

Accordingly, in *The House of Breath* where, among the uncles, aunts, cousins, and a grandmother, he spends his youth, Boy Ganchion asks for the key to his enigmas, a remedy for the kind of solitude which can be relieved only by full self-knowledge. Solitude is the lot of everyone in the "fallen splendid house." Between husbands and wives, between parents and children, there is no accord, no comprehension. Each one remains walled in, gnawed by his vulture and seeking escape. The young have abandoned this household which is too tightly enclosed, as well as the tedium which stifles the small town of Charity. Some have returned—wounded prodigal sons marked by mysterious scars, such as Christy or Folner—in their coffins. Others, like Sue Emma, have lost themselves or, like Ben Berryben, are still trying to find themselves. All of them have been subject to the lure of the *"nourritures terrestres"* in various forms. First it is Bailey's Pasture and the magic grass where enchantments are born. Ernst Robert Curtius (to whom we are indebted for, in addition to the German translation of *The House of Breath*, the first important study of that work) writes:

---

[4] "This Strange, Old World," *New York Times Book Review*, August 20, 1950, p. 17.
[5] *The House of Breath* (New York: Random House, 1950), p. 108.

The herds graze there, and that permits the children of *The House of Breath* to establish contact with animal nature, which, since the Garden of Eden, has been linked to human nature and to which human nature responds. The meadow is full of bitterweeds which seem to have transmitted their bitterness to the milk that has nourished the children. But sometimes these weeds have an effect like that of the enchanted grass that Glaucus ate in the story by Ovid. Seized by an irresistible desire to live in another element, he said goodbye to the earth, to which he was never to return, and dived into the sea, where he suffered a metamorphosis."[6]

Bailey's Pasture is not the only magician. There are also the girl with the lyre who is leaning on the globe and the map which Christy has pinned to the kitchen wall. From these rise the song of the world and the calls from beyond the horizon, voices of sirens which attempt to cover up the appeals coming from the house. For the old people have remained, allowing themselves at best nothing more than the fantasies of the imagination. Malley Ganchion hopes to glimpse a fairyland when she suddenly cracks the shutters of her window. The passage of gypsies or the arrival of a circus causes a flurry of excitement. But these embryonic attempts to escape cannot stand up to the fear of the unknown, the attachment to the soil, and the easygoing charm of idle Sundays on the family veranda. It is necessary then to listen to the chorus of memories, the joy and torment of solitary souls. Malley is obsessed by memories behind her badly fitted shutter. Grandma Ganchion goes down into the cellar to talk with Old Fuzz. The cistern wheel, the echoes in the well, everything conspires for the morose delight of those who are forever alone. Then the plaintive calls resound: "Come home, the light's on, come on home, Ben Berryben. . . . Swimma-a-a! Swimma-a-a! Come in 'fore dark. . . ."

When Boy Ganchion has, with his breath, given the old house the gift of speech, all these calls meet and become intertwined.

Expressed from the second page on, they constitute the frail but distinct framework of the book and allow Goyen to return to the town of Charity as it really was and to trace the story of those who lived there. He does this with a lucidity as pitiless as that of a Jouhandeau, but usually softened by a restrained tenderness much in the manner of Charles-Louis Philippe. The father of Bonne Madeleine and Pauvre Marie would have liked, among others, the story of the good Hattie Clegg and that of poor Jessy.

If William Goyen's novel gave us only some portraits and a tableau of the manners of a small Texas town, even so it would be worth our sympathetic attention. But it contains in addition a study of troubled adolescence, an analysis of the turmoil that accompanies a difficult puberty. Until recent years this theme was rarely chosen by American novelists. Introspection was frowned on. It was thought to indicate a bad tendency toward morbidity, and since the subject was frightening, the writers preferred to leave it aside, or at least to camouflage it. Sherwood Anderson was one of the first to defy the taboos. Erskine Caldwell (especially in *The Sacrilege of Alan Kent*) and William Faulkner fell into step with him. Truman Capote's *Other Voices, Other Rooms* is, in short, merely the exposition of the resolution of a sexual problem, as is, with more pathos and less poetry, William Maxwell's *The Folded Leaf*. In the hands of William Goyen this drama reaches its full intensity.

Each page of *The House of Breath* exudes eroticism. Beginning with the first paragraph the reader is fairly warned: "I went into a public place and saw annunciations drawn and written on the walls." One need not be trained in psychoanalysis in order to discover throughout the book multiple phallic symbols and the constant use of images and rhythms that evoke copulation. Boy Ganchion would have no use for the films and little illustrated manuals which some naïve educators rely on to teach the facts of life to high school boys in his country.

He has chosen nature as his emancipator. If winter, with its snow and ice, shows him the meaning of the word sterility, spring and summer teach him the secrets of fecundation. To dive into the Charity River is to know the pleasure of orgasm. While rising to the surface of the water, Christy and his drowned wife finally consummate their strange marriage.

Christy is the most important of all the characters in *The House of Breath* because he is the most meaningful. He is the medium through whom the powers of Earth work their most disturbing enchantments. He is the Master, the Redeemer, and appears to us as the composite image of Christ and of the Great Pan as Rabelais sketched it four centuries ago in Chapter XXVIII of his Fourth Book. Pan, son of Mercury and Penelope, perhaps, but Pantagruel says:

I consider this Pan to have been the great Saviour of the faithful, Who was ignominiously put to death in Judea by the envy and iniquity of the pontiffs, doctors, priests and monks of the Mosaic law. To me there is nothing abhorrent about this interpretation, for the Saviour can rightly be called Pan in Greek, since He is our All; all that we live, all that we have, all that we hope is Himself, in Him, from Him and by Him. He is the good Pan, the supreme Shepherd Who, as the passionate shepherd Corydon attests, holds in love and affection not only his sheep but also his shepherds.

Those who accept this identification will not be at all astonished that William Goyen has succeeded in doing what at first sight might seem paradoxical: to play, while performing his Priapic rites, only the most Christian and chaste music—fragments of Ecclesiastes, Methodist hymns, and simple proverbs and refrains from folklore.

To this use of all the riches that the primitive spirit bestows on its elect, *The House of Breath* owes its most profound and most original resonances. "The characters," wrote Edwin Muir, "show us another America, as D. H. Lawrence showed

us another England buried beneath the England of the conventional urban imagination."[7] In the same vein, Ernst Robert
Curtius remarks, "We get the impression that we are hearing
the voice of a primitive America which is constantly repressed
by industrial civilization and forced to languish in the colossal
cities."[8] That other primitive, William Faulkner, has sounded
forth this voice many times from the heart of his old dwelling
in Oxford, Mississippi.

It is in Taos, New Mexico, the very place where Lawrence
took refuge, that Goyen has found the retreat where, no longer
annoyed by the acrid smoke of factories, the blaring of loud-
speakers, and the intrigues of literary people, he can listen
to his inner voices while communing with the good earth free
of asphalt. He wrote to me in the month of October:

My garden has gone to seed—seed is sad, somehow, after the bloom—
and our sunflowers have big dried faces like clocks—big as heads. The
sheep are driven down our road, daily, the cattle and horses too, all
down from high country around us to this valley. Magpies are back,
meadowlarks too, and a hundred other kinds of birds are passing over
us every day. This is an enchanted time, the great turning of a season.
I live like a root in dirt—that simple, with that kind of connection. I
am free of the literary world I could not endure, that is not for me.[9]

It seems to me that these few lines say more about *The House
of Breath* than numerous learned commentaries. William Goy-
en's book is not a work of the mind. It is a creation of the heart
and the sense, a great nostalgic song, a painful hymn of love
which could be sung for us only by an artist who is ignorant of
all the kinds of counterfeit money that circulate freely today,
or is too honest to use them even if he knew about them.

---

[7] The English phrasing is mine, translated as directly as possible from
Coindreau's French version. I have been unable to find Muir's review. Coindreau's reference (*The Observer*, London, February 12, 1951) is apparently
erroneous.

[8] Curtius, *loc. cit.*

[9] Letter from El Prado, New Mexico, 1953.

PREFACE TO

*WISE BLOOD**

In presenting *Wise Blood* to the French public, I do not delude myself about the extent of my responsibility and the risks to which I am exposing Miss Flannery O'Connor. There is no question here of a work in which some mere innovations in technique threaten to repel readers inclined to laziness. There are no audacities to shock the prudish. The narrative is lively and fast-paced; it provides an agreeable mixture of horror and comedy, and the unexpected in it keeps the mind constantly alert. Consequently there is no danger of boredom. The danger lies elsewhere, in the very nature of the subject, and the French reader could be excused all the more easily for misinterpreting *Wise Blood* in that he knows nothing—or practically nothing—of the milieu in which this strange story takes place. In actual fact the breed known as evangelists, who are always burlesque, sometimes tragic, and often dangerous, are not a part of our national fauna; hence certain readers may be tempted to denounce the story for improbability and perhaps even to attribute to Flannery O'Connor some sacrilegious and blasphemous intentions which she does not have. For Miss O'Connor is profoundly religious, already classed beside J. F.

* From *La Sagesse dans le sang*, by Flannery O'Connor (Paris: Gallimard, 1959) © Editions Gallimard 1959. Translation by G.M.R.

Powers among Catholic novelists in her country. But it is precisely because she was brought up to respect the inflexible authority of the Church of Rome that she does not trifle with orthodoxy and that she cannot watch, without indignation, amusement, and some pity, the extravagances to which the unrestrained and undirected use of the word of God can lead. Born and still living in Georgia, she finds herself in the middle of the territory of itinerant preachers, for it is chiefly in the states of the South that the evangelistic rabble pullulate—and are seen in the darkest light. The star performers prefer the regions which offer an abundance of important cities and of dollars—the North, the East, and the Midwest. In the West their favorite territory is California.

The evangelists, who appeared as early as the first pioneers, are men and women who go through town and country preaching under the pretext of bringing unbelievers back to God and of reestablishing the reign of virtue on earth. Some of them wander until they die; others, tired of their peregrinations, set up as pastors of some sort of temple, since they always find, in the course of their travels, a confederate who is willing to ordain them. Then they become "Reverends," thus acquiring a degree of social standing. But sometimes their parishioners experience strange surprises when, one fine day, they watch their pastor exchange his Bible for a pair of handcuffs. The evangelists could easily defend themselves by arguing that they are not the only ones to deceive their flocks in such a manner. In February, 1957, to cite only one example, FBI agents discovered that for nine months a certain Calvin Laskey, who had been in trouble with the law since the age of fourteen, had been masquerading, under the name of Dean Barton, as pastor of the Christian Church of Elmdale, Kansas. Arrested for forgery in 1935, he spent some time in a mental hospital, escaped, was arrested for theft in Arizona and Minnesota, and escaped from a prison in Boston in 1945, after having been listed as a deserter in two armies, the Canadian and the American. "The best preacher we've ever had," sighed an old lady of eighty-eight years while watching her spiritual guide move away between two policemen. Hardly a month goes by without a story of some such adventure appearing in the American newspapers.

The evangelists make up a real society which, like every organized society, has its nobility, its bourgeoisie, its poor, and its gangsters. Today the nobility is becoming scarce. Billy Graham, the most recent of the high-flying evangelists, is just a little boy compared with his immediate predecessors, Billy Sunday and Aimee Semple McPherson. But the small fry abound, and just as there is no need today to reach a majority before launching a criminal career, it is no longer necessary in the United States to attain the age of reason in order to preach the word of God. In our day we see young evangelists aged fifteen who began converting the crowds when they were eight years old.

The biographies of the evangelists who achieved fame and rolled in wealth enable us to pick out traits that are common to them all, as we can do with the picaros of Old Spain. Even though Mary Baker Eddy did not belong to the ambulatory type—for she was above all a miracle worker and the founder of a school of healers and of a new religion of the most lucrative sort—I will speak of her nevertheless in the course of this brief study because she possessed, often to the fullest extent, the characteristics of the itinerant soul-saver.

Generally the origins of the evangelists are of the most modest kind. Mary Baker Eddy (1821–1910), although she pretended to be descended from Scottish nobility, was the daughter of a New Hampshire farmer. Billy Sunday (1862–1935) was born on a wretched farm in Iowa, son of a German immigrant named Sonntag who, serving in the army until he was killed, never had a chance to know his son. Aimee Semple McPherson (1890–1944) was also a product of the earth. Her father, a Canadian farmer, belonged to the Methodist Church.

The second point in common is ignorance, the total lack

of culture, even of a primary sort. Mary Baker Eddy could hardly write two coherent sentences and had only the vaguest notion of spelling. But she was clever; and in 1875, at the age of forty-four, after shamelessly pillaging the works of a hypnotizer-healer, Phineas Parkurst Quimby, which she stuffed with quotations from Scripture and references to the teachings of Christ, she succeeded in publishing *Science and Health,* which has since become the bible of her followers.

"This first edition," writes her biographer E. F. Dakin, "was a crude and amateurish piece of writing which bore self-evident contradictions on every page, not to speak of errors in grammar and composition even more striking than those in logic."[1] More competent hands improved the text as time went on.

Billy Sunday too was an ignoramus, and he boasted of that fact. "I don't know any more about theology than a rabbit knows about ping-pong," he told his audiences, who found the statement amusing and became all the more willing to be converted. In his sermons he never missed a chance to aim a few jokes at parents who sent their children to college. Little concerned with the incorrectness of his oratorical style, he could have said what another famous evangelist, Samuel Porter Jones, said: "I deliberately pitch my language to the level of my audience." But it would have been difficult for Billy Sunday to make such an excuse, for Theodore Roosevelt, John D. Rockefeller, Jr., and Secretary of State William Jennings Bryan frequently sat on the platform where he ranted—all of them grateful for the support he gave them in politics and high finance. To preach the love of the flag and the veneration of wealth was to assure himself some precious friendships. President Wilson received him at the White House.

Aimee Semple McPherson (1890–1944) left a reputation at school as an arbitrary but undisciplined child, already an

---

[1] Edwin Franden Dakin, *Mrs. Eddy: The Biography of a Virginal Mind* (New York: Charles Scribner's Sons, 1929), p. 98.

actress. She did not have time to go very far with her studies, for at the age of seventeen she married an ambulant Pentacostal preacher, an exacerbated Holy Roller named Robert Semple, with whom she left for the Orient to evangelize the Chinese. She soon became a widow and returned without a penny but with a month-old baby. Again she married, this time a grocery boy, Samuel McPherson; there was another baby, followed by a divorce. Then the evangelistic tours began.

It should be noted that, particularly among women evangelists, the demon of the flesh awakens quite early, sometimes not without disturbing their nervous systems. Mary Baker Eddy was hysterical from a very early age and remained so until her death. She had attacks of nervousness, convulsions, epilepsy, and catalepsy. She had to be calmed with quantities of morphine, unless she was cradled in the arms of some kind person. The arms of a man were particularly effective. She married three times. First, at the age of twenty, she married George Washington Glover, an apprentice mason who died of yellow fever. Eight years later she became Mary Baker Patterson, having married a handsome dentist who was as well built and vigorous as she could wish. He found himself unable to live with this madwoman, abandoned her, and went off to die in the most dismal misery. Finally, at the age of fifty-six, she entered into her third marriage. This time the husband was Gilbert Eddy, one of her students in Christian Science, son of a farmer and a half-mad mother. After working in a baby carriage factory, he had become a sewing machine salesman. He was a puny fellow and did not grow old. His wife buried him in 1884 and, without going so far as to replace him, entrusted herself to an executive secretary, the very disquieting Calvin Frye. Between these husbands there had been some "students" for whom she had become jealously impassioned. Each of them ran the risk of being pursued later by her merciless hatred.

At the beginning of an evangelistic career we usually find the influence either of a man in the profession (a father, grandfather, or some famous evangelist) or of currently popular theories. Mesmerism and hypnotism penetrated New England when Mary Baker Eddy was still a little girl. In addition she came under the influence of the high priestess of Shaker theology, Ann Lee, who, thinking that God was both man and woman, had changed the beginning of the Lord's Prayer to "Our Father and Mother, which are in Heaven. . . ." Mrs. Eddy adopted this duality, which permitted her, at the peak of her career, to identify herself with the feminine element of the divinity. Her disciple, Mrs. Stetson, even when she had become her rival, never called in question the notion that Mrs. Eddy had descended from Heaven.

In 1886 Billy Sunday, a professional baseball player, having gotten drunk with the members of his team, heard the evangelist Harry Monroe outside the door of the bar bleating some of the hymns that his mother had sung long before on the Iowa farm. That was all it took to start Sunday snapping at the heels of Satan. Since one sect is as good as another, he waited until he was married to decide which one he would join. Two years later he married a Presbyterian, and so he became a Presbyterian. Aimee McPherson was much more precocious. She had hardly been born when her mother, Minnie Kennedy, who had served in the Salvation Army, consecrated her to the service of God. Consequently her first husband had little trouble converting her to the Pentacostal faith that he propagated in his campaigns.

Mary Baker Eddy, as we have said, did not have the temperament for wandering, travel being incompatible with her nervous attacks. She preferred to be given food and lodging in houses where there was an interest in causing tables to move and mediums to speak. When her hosts, pushed to the limit by her extravagances, asked her to go live elsewhere, she sought out other victims to impose herself on until the day when she would again be shown to the door. She never left New England: Lynn, Concord, and Boston were enough for her. For

that matter, why should she have traveled? Most of her followers considered her ubiquitous. In 1909, at the time of the dedication of her Boston temple (an edifice in the form of a cross,
topped by a gigantic crown, and built for the bagatelle of
$1,200,000), the number of the faithful had passed 40,000.
There were 685 branches and 267 societies to help spread
through the world the pretentious nonsense of Mother Eddy,
who, having sold 400,000 copies of *Science and Health,* had
pocketed $500,000 in royalties. And she had quite a few other
sources of revenue.

Billy Sunday and Aimee McPherson were, in some respects,
of a more classic style. In 1893 Billy became the acolyte of one
of the best-known evangelists of the time, J. Wilbur Chapman.
Two years later when Chapman gave up the peripatetic life
in order to become the pastor of a church in Philadelphia,
Billy Sunday did not know what to do. Baseball still tempted
him, but evangelism offered definite possibilities, especially for
a resourceful young man. He had already stolen from his
mentor seven abstracts of sermons (he would steal many others
later; his biographer, William G. McLoughlin, Jr., estimates his
"borrowings" at a minimum figure of 75 percent[2]). He had
good business sense and an unquestionable gift for attracting
crowds; hence he turned himself into a soldier of Christ and
a champion of Americanism. In 1920 his fortune was estimated
at $1,500,000.

Aimee Semple McPherson experienced more difficulty as a
beginner. After returning from the Far East, she drifted from
Maine to Florida, setting up her tent in the most out-of-the-
way places. She sometimes went hungry. Against her were the
scoffers and the strait-laced pastors (because she preached the
joy and pleasure of living), but, without being beautiful, she
had a special appeal. She was tenacious and eloquent, and she
was not handicapped by scruples. Consequently, she won her

[2] *Billy Sunday Was His Real Name* (Chicago: University of Chicago Press,
1955), p. 165.

struggle. In 1918 she arrived in Los Angeles with six dollars and a tambourine, and in 1923 she dedicated the Angelus Temple there, an enormous auditorium that could seat five thousand persons.

That was the mother church of the new sect that she had founded—The International Church of the Foursquare Gospel. When radio developed, she obtained her own broadcasting station; and by 1936, when a census of religious activities was taken in the United States, her church had acquired 205 branches and her followers numbered 16,147.

The success of these quacks of the gospel is to be explained less by their business acumen than by their almost diabolical understanding of their fellow citizens. They know that in the beginning they must win their favor and, while taking care always to appear to be engaged in the saving of souls, relieve their boredom, astonish them with the unexpected, and dazzle them with the external signs of success. Once the evangelist has his audience well in hand, he can deal with them as he likes. There is no absurdity that he cannot make them swallow. Mrs. Eddy's Christian Science, for example, rests entirely on the old Italian evil eye, the medieval belief in spell-casting. If an enemy wishes to do you harm, you immediately fall ill. Mary Baker Eddy calmly denied the existence of matter. She enchanted the corpulent matrons who heard her sermons by saying to them, "Obesity is an adipose belief of yourself as a substance."[3] As a result her most portly disciples took themselves for sylphs. E. F. Dakin remarks incidentally that money was the only thing whose concrete existence Mrs. Eddy never denied. For that and for other reasons, in 1930 the high dignitaries of Christian Science tried to suppress *Mrs. Eddy: The Biography of a Virginal Mind.*

Billy Sunday and Aimee McPherson were infinitely more amusing personages. Billy Sunday introduced the ranting hooligan

[3] Dakin, p. 115.

style into the techniques of evangelism. Sister Aimee played on sex appeal like a virtuoso and capitalized on scandal. The sermons of Billy Sunday were like an act in a Barnum and Bailey circus. The Bible took the place of a baseball. For the benefit of his audiences he translated it into gutter slang, shouted, waved his arms, threw off his coat, jumped off the platform and then remounted it with a perilous leap, seized a chair and smashed it to pieces, declaring that the devil had been sitting there and that it was time to finish with the Prince of Darkness. The audience were ecstatic and readily felt that the Holy Spirit had taken possession of him. Hence they rushed toward this messenger from God and made spectacular professions of faith. They also opened their pocketbooks; for, even though he preached the scorn of money ("There is nobility in poverty," he declared impudently), Billy Sunday had no equal when it came to untying purse strings. One of his methods was to cry, "Everyone who is willing to give a dollar, stand up!" At that very moment the small orchestra of cornets and trombones which accompanied him would begin playing the national anthem. Automatically the audience rose to their feet. Actually, Billy Sunday was above all a recruiting sergeant for the Protestant denominations who gave him their financial support. His converts were immediately sent to join the most generous sects. For certain pastors the Reverend Mr. Sunday was a good investment, and each one derived a profit from him. Unfortunately the conversions were not always in fast colors. When Billy had moved on and the hysteria had calmed, the neophytes backslid. The churches gradually emptied and the pastors realized that investments in the stock market would have paid more substantial dividends. This fact helps to explain Billy Sunday's decline after the triumphal year of 1917, when he came to sweep the impurities from New York while celebrating the entrance of the United States into the war.

Aimee Semple McPherson, aided by her honorable mother, Minnie Kennedy, was just as successful in her enterprise. Her methods were different. She did not have the aid of the Protestant churches because she did not provide them with converts. She kept them for herself. In 1936 her followers exceeded fifteen thousand. She treated them quite well, offering them, in addition to the salvation of their souls, many kinds of diversion. Her personal charms came first: provocative Venetian-blond hair, done up in a pyramid; evangelical but suggestive gowns, made by the best couturiers; and warm, persuasive eloquence. But her highest trump was the live tableau. The whole Biblical story was revived that way, according to the taste of the day. In our day she undoubtedly would have organized striptease shows to recreate the horror of Salome letting her seventh veil fall at the feet of Herod. Her audacity was unlimited. This fact was clearly seen when, at Ocean Park where she had gone to swim on May 18, 1926, she disappeared. It was believed that she had drowned. On the fatal beach, engravings were sold that showed her walking on the water, like Christ, Bible in hand, a huge flower on her bodice, en route to Paradise. She was indeed en route, but her destination was a small cottage at Carmel (several miles south of San Francisco), where she was awaited by the former operator of her private radio station, Kenneth G. Ormiston, a lame, somewhat bald, but otherwise attractive fellow. While Aimee was relaxing thus from her evangelistic fatigue, Mama Kennedy took over the divine services and organized a colossal drive for funds to build a sumptuous mausoleum in honor of her daughter. Money came pouring in. Between fits of crying, Minnie kept the accounts. This is when the vaudeville show began.[4] On May 25 the public learned that it was not the Lord who had called away the most beautiful of his servants, but some bandits who, having kidnapped her and taken her to Mexico, demanded $500,000 for her release. Immediately, religious services were held in the Angelus Temple to raise money for the ransom.

[4] For a day-by-day account see Lately Thomas, *The Vanishing Evangelist* (New York: Viking, 1959). M.E.C.

June 23 the victim reappeared in the United States and told the story of her escape through a desert full of cactus and wild beasts. But, because she was as fresh as a rose and did not even have dust on her shoes, a few skeptical minds suspected fraud. The police took charge of the affair, and for seven months the American press spread before its readers everything that the dregs of a nation can offer when brought to the surface. Aimee McPherson, driven to the most flagrant lies, bought false witnesses who later retracted their testimony. Judges like those in a Courteline play floundered in imbroglios that would have frightened Feydeau. For the sake of peace and quiet, on January 10, 1927, the exhausted court dismissed the entire rabble. Sister Aimee had worn them out. The next day she began a triumphal tour through the United States. Not for a moment had she lost her bearings or forgotten her duties as the daughter of Jesus Christ (a title that she was pleased to confer on herself). The interrogations were hardly finished when she began retracing, for the benefit of the faithful, in tableaux more alive than ever, the stages of her calvary. The best of these pantomimes was "The March of the Martyrs," presented October 3, 1926, before more than 40,000 ecstatic persons. At the back of the scene stood an enormous cross upon which, to conclude the spectacle, skillfully placed lights projected the shadow of Aimee McPherson, with her eyes toward the skies and her arms extended. The year 1926 was the apogee of this publicity genius. Her death on September 20, 1944, caused little stir. Nevertheless, she still had disciples, and it is told that some soldiers on duty in Europe requested leave to attend Sister Aimee's funeral. History does not say whether they were boys for whom, in the course of her tours, she had done favors.

But now we must approach the heroes of Flannery O'Connor, and for that we must descend the social ladder. What do we find? Small-time evangelists who, unable to afford the luxury of temples and tabernacles accommodating thousands of persons, continue the old tradition of tents which they set up close to villages and to which they lure their victims with Bible reading, baptisms, and often with miracles of healing. They are sometimes arrested for the illegal practice of medicine. Thus in Miami in 1956 the police interrupted the career of a certain Jack Coe, an evangelist of the Assembly of God. He had to admit to the court that in five years he had amassed the nice little sum of $500,000.[5]

Most of the small-time traveling evangelists limit themselves to more modest returns. They form a veritable court of miracles which swarms with—among a few visionaries—ex-convicts, swindlers, perverts, and lunatics of every sort. Their ancestors date back to the early nineteenth century. Beginning in 1802 an ambulant preacher named Grenade introduced shouting revivals into the Southern states. After a while at these gatherings the audiences would begin to shout—a sign, according to this man of God, that the Holy Spirit was starting to speak. After an hour or two it spoke so vigorously that everyone made for the bushes and thickets in a sexual frenzy that made Bacchanalias and Priapic rites look like children's games. This kind of "revival" later facilitated the swindling activities of the famous Methodist evangelist-bandit, John Murrel, who waited until his audiences were in a trance before selling them slaves whom he had stolen from their owners, and passing off counterfeit money as change. When moving from one meeting place to another, he would stop travelers on the road, kill them, split them open and remove the insides as in cleaning a chicken, fill the bodies with rocks and sand, sew them up, and throw them into a river, whence there was no danger they would return. All this is a long way from the evangelist analyzed by Alphonse Daudet.

Since the low-level evangelistic sharpers are infinitely more complex and colorful, they appear more often in the American novel than do the millionaire swindlers, whose motives and methods are easy enough to dismantle. One book, nevertheless, evokes Billy Sunday and Aimee McPherson. That is Sinclair Lewis's famous *Elmer Gantry*. Also there is more than a little resemblance between Aimee McPherson and Edith Flemming, heroine of *The Evangelist*, a mediocre novel by Howard Otway.[6] But we must turn to the Southern novelists to learn what is to be found in the dirty waters of the lower forms of evangelism which they have constantly before their eyes. From these waters they draw either the central theme of their novels or some of the characters, men and women who are avaricious, debauched, and generally comical in a way that lends itself easily to caricature.

It will be recalled that in William Faulkner's *As I Lay Dying* Jewel is the child of the sin that Addie, his mother, has committed with Brother Whitfield. The latter, visiting the house of the dying Addie with the intention of asking Anse, the husband, to forgive him is content to murmur, like a good Tartuffe, "God's grace upon this house." The Lord in his mercy will accept, he thinks, the intention in place of the deed. I will also point out Sister Ida, whom Truman Capote parades in her truck with her fifteen children—some of them adopted, others having different fathers whose names she does not know—one of them being Little Homer Honey, the child cowboy-evangelist who is advertised as follows: "Let Little Homer Honey Lasso Your Soul For The Lord."[7] Readers of Caldwell's *Tobacco Road* have not forgotten Sister Bessie, the nymphomaniac evangelist, her marriage with young Dude, and the hotel where she spends the night running from one room to another. In addition, Erskine Caldwell gave us *Journeyman,* in which Semon Dye siphons off the money of the husbands whose wives and daughters he violates and organizes shouting revivals in the manner of the Reverend Mr. Grenade. We should place this edifying character beside the sinister Harry Powell in *The*

---

[6] Howard Otway, *The Evangelist* (New York: Harper, 1954).
[7] *The Grass Harp* (New York: Random House, 1951), p. 107.

Night of the Hunter, by Davis Grubb.[8] Having learned that two children know the hiding place of a treasure that their father concealed before being hanged, Powell pursues them with the Bible in one hand and a dagger in the other, in order to make them, under torture if necessary, tell him the secret. The story takes place in West Virginia.

But until Flannery O'Connor began to write, the evangelists had never found anyone who could appreciate them at their true value and depict them as they deserve to be depicted. *Wise Blood* and most of the stories in the collection *A Good Man Is Hard to Find* finally get to the bottom of the subject.

Born in Savannah in 1926, Flannery O'Connor studied at Georgia State College for Women, at Milledgeville, and then at the University of Iowa, where she took courses under Paul Engle. Forced to live in the country because of her health, she resides with her mother, Mrs. Regina Cline O'Connor, on a huge estate a few miles from Milledgeville. She has read relatively little: her interest in spiritual problems inclines her toward work in depth rather than toward the dispersion of surface matters. Dilettantism is not to her liking. With this attitude she has achieved a maturity of mind and a seriousness which I have hardly found in anyone else except William Goyen, who is ten years her senior. Hence it was inevitable that she turn her attention to those who make a game of what is dearest to her heart and that she scourge them properly. She was thus led to present the world in a form whose violence certifies its sincerity. She remarks:

. . . For me the meaning of life is centered in our Redemption by Christ and . . . what I see in the world I see in its relation to that. . . .

. . . .

My own feeling is that writers who see by the light of their Christian faith will have, in these times, the sharpest eyes for the grotesque, for

[8] Davis Grubb, *The Night of the Hunter* (New York: Harper, 1953).

the perverse, and for the unacceptable. . . . Redemption is meaning-
less unless there is cause for it in the actual life we live, and for the
last few centuries there has been operating in our culture the secular
belief that there is no such cause.

The novelist with Christian concerns will find in modern life distortions which are repugnant to him, and his problem will be to make
these appear as distortions to an audience which is used to seeing them
as natural; and he may well be forced to take ever more violent means
to get his vision across to this hostile audience. When you can assume
that your audience holds the same beliefs you do, you can relax a little
and use more normal ways of talking to it; when you have to assume
that it does not, then you have to make your vision apparent by shock
—to the hard of hearing you shout, and for the almost blind you draw
large and startling figures.[9]

In the light of this quotation, I do not believe we can mistake the interpretation that should be given to *Wise Blood.* In
the tragicomic world of these evangelists—Asa Hawks, the
man who fakes blindness, Onnie Jay Holy, the guitar player,
and the visionary Hazel Motes (the only sincere one in this
madness to which his heresy has brought him) —we find only
sacrilegious caricatures. There Christ takes on the form of a
mummy, and the tabernacle becomes a vanity table. Everything is debased and grotesque. To describe this world, Flannery O'Connor has found the only language that would be
appropriate, a kind of melancholy humor, allied with a direct-
ness which fears neither words nor scenes. "Miss O'Connor's
style," William Goyen has written, "is tight to choking and as
direct and uncompounded as the order to a firing squad to
shoot a man against a wall."[10]

Miss O'Connor has just finished a new novel whose title, *The
Violent Bear It Away,* comes from the Gospel according to
St. Matthew (11:12) : "From the days of John the Baptist until
now, the kingdom of heaven suffereth violence, and the violent

[9] "The Fiction Writer and His Country," in *The Living Novel: A Symposium,* ed. Granville Hicks (New York: Macmillan, 1957) , pp. 162–63.
[10] "Unending Vengeance," *New York Times Book Review,* May 18, 1952,
p. 4.

bear it away." Here again we find a false prophet of the type of Hazel Motes's grandfather. Neither the humor nor the tightness of the writing has relented in the least. The wealth of inventiveness is still there, as well as the originality of vision. This third book only confirms the talent—remarkable in her generation—of the author, a reserved young woman who is too modest and always a little hesitant when questioned about her work. She prefers to talk about her leisure activities, painting and the raising of peacocks. Thirty of these noisy birds decorate the terraces and lawns of the family estate where she lives apart from all publicity. She takes pleasure in studying their habits, in observing their combat tactics or the delightful arabesques of their hide-and-seek games among the shrubbery. At sunset they fly to the branches of the cedars bordering the poultry yard. The Georgia landscape then becomes a Japanese landscape, and the very sight of these magnificent creatures lined against the sky in the fading light makes it possible for Miss O'Connor to go on believing in the beauty and sweetness of life.

PREFACE TO

*THE FOLDED LEAF**

It would ill become me to deny, since I myself am partly responsible, that there exists today in France a stereotype of American literature. It is thought that everything has been said when one affirms that this literature belongs to a young country where everyone believes it is idle to split hairs while so many immediate goals must be attained. It is said that the American is hostile to meditation and suspicious of dreams, not because of an incapacity to dream or to meditate, but because he dreads the self-confrontation that would make him conscious of the solitude to which he is condemned. The causes of this solitude are economic and social for some, psychological for others. On the one hand, there are the defects of a political system which favors inequality and tolerates injustices (racial prejudice, among others); on the other, there are the tight-lipped puritan grandmothers standing guard while, in the distance on the rocks revealed by the sea, the sirens sing without letting themselves be intimidated. One must choose between surrender and struggle. In both cases the victim will be tortured. Consequently, the American novel is a tormented novel, written, by definition, in hasty and brutal language, devoid of

* From *La Feuille repliée,* by William Maxwell (Paris: Gallimard, 1948) © Editions Gallimard 1948. Translation by G.M.R.

nuances and subtleties. If an author does not fit this stereotype, rather than change the stereotype, a commentator will seize upon traits in the author's work which seem to confirm the preconceived ideas. Thus everyone is satisfied: the critics, who do no more than repeat what they have already said a hundred times; and the public, which, comfortably installed with its little habits, knows very well that it is not being disturbed.

But matters are not so simple. The stereotype of American literature, like all stereotypes for that matter, is based on truth, but it is a partial truth which explains only a group of works whose noisiness drowns out musical tones of too intimate a character to be perceived by deafened or simply inexperienced ears. The literature of a nation is like an orchestra in that it has its brasses and percussion instruments, and also its violins and flutes. The loudest instruments make the first impression. They cannot be ignored by anyone, not even the stone deaf. The other instruments demand more attention, more alert senses, a more delicate ability to listen. Is this to say that they are inferior to the instruments that blare? To answer in the affirmative would be to maintain that in a symphony the strings are less important than the trumpets, and the horns are inferior to the cymbals—an obvious absurdity.

In the case of American literature the error is all the more flagrant in that the preponderance of brass is of relatively recent date. It is a postwar development beginning somewhere around 1920. (The first naturalists were actually still timid with their audacities.) Americans had not awaited the representatives of what Gertrude Stein called the "lost generation" in order to busy themselves with works of the mind. One forgets too easily that Emerson and Melville were Americans, just as were Thoreau, the solitary walker, Hawthorne, so skilled in veiling human baseness, and Henry James with his subtle complexities. Around these major figures gravitated a number of sensitive writers who, neglected today by the general public, are devoutly admired by small groups of literati immunized

against infatuations or passing enthusiasms. I did not say indifferent to the current vogue, for it is precisely toward these
authors who have been long abandoned that the vogue of today
seems to be oriented. Henry James has been restored to a place
of honor, and one is no longer afraid to discover first-rate qualities in very simple stories, tales made of trifles, such as the
charming vignettes of Sarah Orne Jewett, who was presented
by her translator, Marie-Thérèse de Solms Blanc, under the
pseudonym Th. Bentzon, to the French public in 1885.

The literature of that period was not the literature of a
young country, no doubt because it came into being in a very
industrious territory where men matured quickly and found
enough leisure (not being able to turn on the radio) to listen
to their inner voices and (not being able to go to the movies) to
be moved by the daily tragedies which their lives presented
without the addition of revolvers, gin, or whiskey. The present
stereotype of American literature, then, is to be explained
partly by a lack of perspective and by ignorance of the fact
that the youthfulness of a country is a cyclical phenomenon,
periods of infantilism being always preceded—and happily
followed—by periods of maturity. It is the function of a few
authors to act as a bridge and, in the fullness of juvenile
effervescence, to retain a sense of measure, of the serene im-
partiality that is indispensable to anyone wishing to paint life
exactly and to analyze men dispassionately.

William Maxwell today seems to me the very type of the
"linking" author through whom tradition is perpetuated, enriched by new contributions. He has the seriousness of the
great nineteenth-century writers, as well as the tact, the reserve, and the respect for his art. On the other hand, he resembles his contemporaries in that he has none of the old false
modesty. He knows how to be crude and violent when these
qualities are needed, but he does not make them into a duty
or a mystique. He is aware of all the most recent discoveries
of psychiatry, and if he cleans wounds by surgery, he does it

with a sure scalpel. Indifferent to Hollywood subjects and techniques, he has not succumbed to gangster romanticism; and his sensibility, in which the lightest abrasion can arouse painful resonances, frees him from the necessity of roving around bars, slums, and battlefields in search of outcasts, victims, and heroes. It is enough for him to pull back the corner of a curtain in a very ordinary American cottage, to listen to the heart of a child or an adolescent, to look at a mother and her son or at a woman and her husband or lover. It is thus that he finds his tragedies, which are latent and silent, and therefore infinitely more moving than the spectacular crimes of the "tough school" of novelists. I thought of Maxwell a few days ago while reading the following lines by Valery Larbaud, who was meditating over a work by some writer of the Céline type:

A great deal of wind and much noise—that is the memory I retain from this reading. Yet the author has talent, know-how, and skill, and he has certainly done his best to rouse me and, if not to convince me, at least to irritate me. Every page offers words that are considered crude and obscene and that are not usually seen in print; from time to time there are filthy insults addressed to famous people, social groups, institutions, and establishments such as the police, the army, the government, the clergy. . . . Having left this noisy territory, I took up another book in which, from the earliest phrases, I recognized human substance and intonation, just as I should have recognized at once in the first book the lack of substance and the coldness of another sort of academism. Without seeking for effects, with no other artifice than a closely woven tissue of accurate little details and of precise words . . . the author of this book kept me interested and involved, in a state of eager anticipation. And when at last, to my regret, I was through reading, I realized that of the two books the truly revolutionary one, the subversive one, was the second, the simple, unpretentious but genial work of a woman about whom I know nothing except that her name is Gianna Manzini and that she lives in Florence. But I know very well that Charles-Louis Philippe would have liked what she writes.[1]

[1] *Sous l'Invocation de Saint Jérôme* (Paris: Gallimard, 1946), p. 169.

Replace Gianna Manzini with William Maxwell and Florence with Yorktown Heights, and the quotation applies to the author of *The Folded Leaf* without a single word needing to be changed.

He was born in 1908 in Lincoln, a town of twelve thousand inhabitants in Illinois. He lived there until the age of fifteen and then moved to Chicago. His education was that of every young American who wishes to acquire a solid cultural foundation—high school and four years of college. He spent the college years at the University of Illinois and then went to Harvard to begin study toward a doctorate. From 1931 to 1933 he continued doctoral study at the University of Illinois, where he had returned to teach freshman English. During this period he read intensively. He discovered medieval French literature with enchantment, and he made contact with the authors who were to provide his bedside reading: Dostoevsky, Flaubert, Alain Fournier, E. M. Forster, Virginia Woolf. A stay in New York was followed by two years of travel. Then he worked for ten years as a writer for the *New Yorker* before retreating to the calm of a country lane where he writes and dreams among his wife and his favorite cats in a small cottage surrounded by apple trees.

His ancestors, whose lineage he can trace back to the eighteenth century, have bequeathed him English, Scottish, Welsh, French, German, and Dutch blood. One of them, Jonathan Harrington, was the first victim of the American Revolution. More recently the men in Maxwell's family have tended to be lawyers—both his grandfathers and then both his brothers. But various members of the family are also musicians. One of his grandfathers gave singing lessons, and his father was well enough versed in harmony to compose a Scottish dance for orchestra. Maxwell himself, passionately fond of music (especially of opera), lived for a while on a farm in Wisconsin in daily contact with one of the most famous pianists in America, Josef Lhevinne.

His mother preferred painting and embroidery to music. This extremely refined and exquisitely sensitive woman died when her son William was ten years old. Her death was more to the child than the loss of someone tenderly cherished. It was the collapse of a whole world to which he clung with every fiber of his innermost being. This world is never out of Maxwell's thoughts. He likes to analyze it, to recall its gentleness and charm. One day he said to me:

My love of European culture is just like that of my grandparents, who were contemporaries of Henry James. Less privileged than he, they were nevertheless subconsciously troubled by the nostalgia that all sensitive people felt in those days. Their fathers and their mothers, being pioneers, had enough to do just to make their life secure. After the Civil War, order and security were quickly established, but the new civilization was essentially materialistic and commercial and offered nothing to people with imagination. They suffered from it, they recalled old memories, they felt the attraction and the need for artistic things; and art, for almost all of them (and no doubt they were right), was to be found in Europe. I never knew either of my grandparents, but one of my aunts had gone to the Continent on her honeymoon. To decorate her house she had brought back some reproductions of paintings and some photographs of things like the Coliseum and the Bridge of Sighs. She had also brought back a name for her horse, which she called Dreyfus. I remember too how some friends of Scottish origin received a visit one day by a lady who had come directly from Scotland. That was an important event in our town. Now, our families had been American for a good hundred years, but since it was not possible to cross the ocean in a few days as it would be about two generations later, everything that was handed down from our ancestors, the smallest fact, the most insignificant tradition, was carefully held in trust. In such things, we found the color that embellished the rather unromantic environment in which we were forced to live. Naturally, we accepted innovations that added to our comfort, but in a small town such as Lincoln the middle class were serious about not breaking with the past, and they took care not to let the houses lose the personality given them by the great-grandparents who had built them.[2]

[2] Since the only record of Maxwell's statement is Coindreau's version in French, the phrasing of the "quotation" presented here is mine, not Maxwell's.

All the poetry of heroic faraway times, William Maxwell found incarnated in his mother. When she was dead, and the house was sold, the family dispersed. Nothing remained but ruins and, alone among them, a young romantic whose soul was constricted by nostalgia. It is this nostalgia (similar in kind to that which makes its way so often into the novels of William Faulkner and other Southern writers) which explains not only the subjects that William Maxwell generally deals with, but also the emotion which emanates from their apparent simplicity. His novels and short stories are a patient, sensitive effort to reconstitute people and times that have passed. To that end he uses family scenes in houses where life runs a full and normal course. There is such a house in *They Came Like Swallows* (1937) [3]; it is a reproduction of the one in Lincoln where the author spent his childhood. In these dwellings, traditions are respected. All anniversaries are celebrated, and Thanksgiving, Christmas, and Easter are honored with no change in the rituals that have been established for many generations. Around the mother and father the children fret and quarrel; uncles, aunts, and cousins gather at the slightest incident. I hasten to say that these are not edifying stories in the manner of the Comtesse de Ségur. Maxwell does not specialize in the study of monsters and dramas of dissolution, but he nevertheless knows that virtue is not commonplace. He attempts to show the sadness of life rather than to exploit its horrors. If his children (whom he analyzes with rare perfection) are never odious, the reason is that he knows how to make us feel the depths of suffering sometimes reached by this "age without pity."

Driven from the paradise of Lincoln, Illinois, Maxwell found refuge in the university, which henceforth would be the reference point of his thoughts in somber hours. Of this other paradise—so very different from the family sanctuary—he could not fail to expose the inmost elements, to make its hidden soul

---

[3] In 1937 this book was selected by the **Book-of-the-Month Club** and was awarded a prize by the Friends of American Writers. M.E.C.

rise to view. In 1945 he published *The Folded Leaf,* which today I offer to French readers under the title *La Feuille repliée.*

I have indicated elsewhere the importance of college life in the American novel.[4] At the age of five the American child begins his education. After a year of kindergarten he enters primary school, which may be public or private. Around the age of fourteen he advances to spend four years in high school (free and administered by the city) or to a preparatory school (independent but not free). Some at the age of eighteen consider their education finished and set out to earn their living; others, aspiring to a higher education, take the college entrance examinations. After four years they come out of college with a diploma that is equivalent, *grosso modo,* to a *licence* or a *diplôme d'études supérieures. The Folded Leaf* traces the lives of a group of boys and girls during the high school and college years.

A complete knowledge of university milieux, memories of his own experiences, and a special talent for psychology have enabled William Maxwell to write the only novel which, to my knowledge, gives an exact picture of college life in the United States. Many writers had attempted this feat before him, one of them being Scott Fitzgerald with his very famous *This Side of Paradise.* But their works, written prematurely, only grazed the surface of a terrain particularly difficult to explore; and like all works based on unripe and badly assimilated experience, they soon became dated. Maxwell allowed *The Folded Leaf* to gestate for ten years, and he wrote four versions of it. Consequently, the study which he has given us seems to me definitive. Through a particular case he has arrived at the general. The drama of Lymie, Spud, and Sally is not restricted to the University of Illinois. It is a drama of all places and all times, the drama of young persons who have not yet learned how to dis-

---

[4] See the two-part essay on this subject in this volume.

cover the secrets of their own hearts. No doubt some readers will find Spud and Lymie strangely naïve. Even more surely they will doubt the innocence of the relations between the two boys and will be tempted to conclude that *The Folded Leaf* presents a case of homosexuality. They will be wrong. Never during their intimacy do the two friends suspect that their attachment could be based on something which they could contemplate only with horror. They love each other with the ingenuousness of boys who have never been disturbed by the mysteries of the subconscious, and when, in the cold dormitory, they sleep in each other's arms in plain sight of all their comrades, they do so with no more perversity than the child who insists on going to bed at night with the teddy bear that he adores. Today, with the vulgarization of Freudianism, the growing freedom of the written and spoken word, and the boldness of the barracks humor that is current from the Atlantic to the Pacific, so much ingenuousness would be very improbable; but during the period when this fine love story, *The Folded Leaf,* takes place (in a small town in the Midwest) the severity of the formidable taboos had not yet been relaxed. Hence, in order for the tragedy to have the ring of truth, it had to be reproduced for us just as the actors played it. In their view, however, there was never any question of sexual anomaly, although they undoubtedly knew that such things existed, without for a moment envisaging the possibility that they themselves could one day become involved.

The dominant influence of the past on Maxwell enabled him, during the long gestation of *The Folded Leaf,* to regain the freshness of his emotions in adolescence, while the detachment and the maturity of mind which had come with age gave him the composure and objectivity necessary for his perilous analyses. As a result, we have before us a novel that would seem to have been written at once by a young man still vibrant with the drama he had just witnessed and by a psychologist called in consultation much later to insure that everything be brought into focus, judged, and evaluated without the distorting interference of a sensibility that becomes vulnerable too easily.

The devotion to the past,[5] which gives rise to the restrained melancholy that envelopes every one of Maxwell's works, is also the source of the satire which, with cunning irony, he places like a comic mask on the tragic face of everyday life. One should read his first novel, *Bright Center of Heaven* (1934), in order to sample the kind of humor practiced around 1930 by a whole group of writers in the wake of Norman Douglas and Ronald Firbank. Today Maxwell judges this initial work very severely. He is embarrassed by the influences that can be seen in it. On this point, I think, he is over-scrupulous. *Bright Center of Heaven*, with its lyrical theme handled in a comic manner, is a very funny novel, full of wit and worthy of close study if only as a means to a better understanding of *They Came Like Swallows*. A parallel examination of these two books will bring out the contrast between two families and two ways of life, one of which, because of its absurdity, arouses the satiric spirit, while the other piously evokes memories that have defied time. Hence the difference in tone. In *Bright Center of Heaven* it is exceptional for the irony to permit a few brief flashes of emotion. In *They Came Like Swallows* the veiled tenderness is enlivened only incidentally by darts of humor.

One can see how William Maxwell's books differ radically from the tough novels that are wrongly considered as the very essence of American literature. They differ just as much in form. Here there is no attempt to create special effects in style or in scene. A musician like his father and grandfather, Maxwell knows what can be achieved with a sordino. A painter and embroiderer like his mother, he executes petit point tapestries in which the most vivid colors end by dissolving in subtle gradations. So great is his fear of garishness that sometimes, not finding tints

---

[5] The months he spent on a farm in Wisconsin inspired him, while he was alone in Martinique, to write a charming story, "The Heavenly Tenants" (1946). M.E.C.

discreet enough to translate his thought, he practices reticence and suggestion rather than direct indication. One could say of him what Julian Green, in the third book of his *Journal,* says of Nathaniel Hawthorne: "What makes him important to me is, above all, the value he places on silence and on everything invisible. His is a solitary, mysterious soul, closer to night than to day." Maxwell has attained such virtuosity in expressing the invisible that he has even used it as the theme of a story, "The Intruders" (not yet published). It is so abstract that one wanders in the same shadows where the characters struggle isolated in worlds ringed with watertight compartments whose entrances are mutually forbidden.

William Maxwell's novels are not written for the multitude, and undoubtedly when they become known in France they will surprise those who have somewhat hastily formed a two-dimensional image of America in black and white, punctuated with crude exclamations, gunfire, the smashing of bottles, and the cries of raped women and lynched Negroes. That America exists, but one could live from birth to death on American soil without ever having any evidence of it. Consequently, the literature that depicts it is as fragmentary as a sociological document can be. If we except the work of a Dos Passos or of a William Faulkner, this literature is somehow detached from the soil that gave it birth, hardly touching down at more than one point. The books that depict such a brutish America are colored by the times in which they were written. That is what we must understand about them so that we will not exaggerate their importance. A Hemingway, a Caldwell, a Steinbeck have done no more than give expression to a few *tics douloureux* in the face of America. It was unavoidable that these writers be made known to us, since they contract the muscles and make the nerves cry out; but I believe that it is preferable to seek the real face of the nation, the habitual face, the one which reveals the deep ancestral nature and the secret personality of America, in the work of a William Maxwell.

PART FOUR

THE AMERICAN COLLEGE NOVEL

COLLEGE LIFE

AND THE AMERICAN NOVEL

PART ONE: 1920–1945*

The one we see every day is a schoolboy with unkempt hair, poorly informed, corrupted by some common vice which has already destroyed in him the sacredness of primary ideals. Or if, miraculously, the poor child has escaped that plague of the schools, it is impossible that he has preserved the chastity of his imagination and the sacred ignorance appropriate to his age.

—George Sand

If it is true that literature sometimes influences manners, it is even more true that manners always influence literature. Consequently there are some genres that properly belong to certain countries and become acclimated in others only with great difficulty. Thus France ranks in the first category of nations that have a military novel. Still embryonic in the work of Balzac (for *Les Chouans* is primarily a war novel, and "Une Passion dans le désert" is only a short story), the novel of military life flowered at the end of the nineteenth century, when the democratic spirit imposed compulsory military service on all citizens regardless of rank or fortune. Further, that flowering was greatly

* From "La Vie de collège et le roman américain," in *Aperçus de littérature américaine* (Paris: Gallimard, 1946), pp. 32–49. © Editions Gallimard 1946. Translation by G.M.R.

facilitated by the interest that the realists and the naturalists, then all-powerful, brought immediately to this most sordid aspect of French life. In the military quarters they could study at their leisure those old instincts which their scalpels delighted so much in exposing. Here they saw the beast wallowing in the stale smell of the barracks. For them the soldier became the equal of the prostitute. And Lucien Descaves was able to write *Sous-Offs.*

One would search in vain for works of this type in American literature, just as one could not find penetrating studies of bawdy-houses. In time of peace American youth experience neither military servitude nor military grandeur. And if they experience fleshly love, they do so only on the sly; for prostitution, being illegal, is considered, ipso facto, as nonexistent. What is more, that fact does not prevent it from showing its wares on every streetcorner, but eyes see only what one wants to let them see. As soon as the law has said no, morality is safe and this fine Uncle Sam can dare to give old Europe some lessons in virtue without too much fear that people will laugh in his face. One had to wait for Stephen Crane, with *Maggie, A Girl of the Streets* (1893), and later Theodore Dreiser in order to see the woman of easy virtue become a type of character in novels. She is still nothing more than an isolated heroine. In many novels one finds bawdyhouse episodes, but to my knowledge there is still no book in American literature comparable to *La Fille Elisa, La Maison Tellier,*[1] or Kuprin's *Yama (The Pit)*.

On the other hand, the system of education which consists of instructing men and women for four years in magnificent colleges has given the United States a whole class of novels that France would never dream of writing. The lycée and the university scarcely affect the life of the French citizen. There he takes several courses pointing toward the inevitable exami-nations and at four o'clock goes home. There is no communal

---

[1] Novels by the Goncourt brothers (1877) and by Maupassant (1881), in the order given.

life as in the American colleges, and no individuality among our faculties, on whom the State enforces a uniformity which includes the program of studies. We have none of that naïve but touching love that Americans show for their *alma mater*, for these shady campuses where each summer at commencement time white-haired old gentlemen come, generally quite drunk, to listen with tears in their eyes to the songs that evoke their youth.

The American has two countries: his homeland and his college. He is American, but he is also a Harvard man, a Yale man, a Princeton man. And a feeling of intransigent superiority accompanies this miniature nationalism, a feeling which gives rise to jealousies, grudges, and sometimes even real declarations of war. Every college is in effect a little republic. A president sits at the summit, surrounded by deans who form the council of ministers. Then come the corps of professors, officials of more or less importance, and several thousand subjects, the students. Depending on the place, the latter can be all of one sex or mixed. Every college has its colors and its anthem. It also has its army, the football team. It is the football team that undertakes, in the various stadiums of the region, to defend the national honor. The level of scholarship accounts for only a part of the reputation of a college. The best college is the one whose team has beaten all the others, and the enrollment figures grow in proportion to the athletic success because a father will take a second look before placing his son in a college that lists only defeats. Let us not cry scandal! Is not the greatness of a country measured by the valor of its army rather than by the merit of its writers? The sword takes precedence over the pen, and men are always proud of the victories won by their country. The American college has its courts and its legislative assemblies in which professors and students are represented. It has its newspapers, its theaters, its poor and its rich, its respectable people, and its rowdies—all of which necessitates a police force and a strictly enforced code.

Naturally, these little democracies offer the advantages and the disadvantages inherent in such regimes. In his annual report for 1937 one of the deans of Princeton University, Christian Gauss, faces the problem squarely:

It is idle to pretend that democracy is either the simplest or the most expeditious form of government. Government by ukase is far simpler and calls for less expenditure of time and effort. We must be willing to face these disadvantages with patience and reduce them where possible. But the great advantages of democracy are not to be sought on the administrative side. They are to be found only in the long run and in the immense gain in general morale and in the self-respect of all members of the community in which the processes of cooperative government prevail. Crises in democratically governed communities are most likely to occur where there is lack of acquaintance, understanding, and good will between the component parts of that society. So long as students and professors consider themselves as distinct orders of society with antagonistic interests, possible causes of friction are certain to be numerous and constant.

This is why at Princeton, at least, the barriers between professors and students have been removed for the greater good of both groups. In close contact with his masters, the student not only realizes that he is no longer a child, but his work becomes a kind of friendly collaboration and consequently is more interesting and profitable. For his part, the professor in constant touch with young people retains a freshness of mind that delays the inevitable day when academic routine will turn him into a pontificating fossil. The stream where everyone goes rowing, the path where everyone goes walking, the tavern where everyone fraternizes—these often do more for teaching than the classroom with its professorial chair and its desks.

Such, in outline, is the small republic of which the young American upon leaving preparatory school around the age of eighteen will become a citizen for four years. He is still a child when he arrives. He is a grown man when he leaves. He looks on life with the assurance of the Frenchman who returns from his regiment. And if he has a literary inclination, he does not fail to publish a novel about that university life which, for better or for worse, enabled him to find himself.

This explains the profusion of college novels in current American literature, at a time when they are the exception in French literature. Only a few of our great schools, those with a pronounced individuality, have furnished the novelist with themes. I am thinking of the Ecole Normale as M. Abel Hermant has described it in his first novel, *Monsieur Rabosson,* and the Ecole de Sèvres in *Sévriennes,* by Gabrielle Réval.

It is extremely difficult to classify novels about college life. If some of them show very definite characteristics there are others of a nature that is hard to determine. All are fundamentally subjective, often prejudiced, and always partial; and it must be acknowledged that there are no really good ones. This lack can be explained by the difficulty of the subject and by its extensiveness. "It would take an entire *Human Comedy* to describe Princeton," André Maurois remarked to me one day. But Princeton is the smallest of the great American universities, and André Maurois had lived there for only three months. Consequently he was not acquainted with all the mysterious inner life of the place, with all the secret intrigues that would have to be brought to life in order to draw a significant picture. Since every college puts its special stamp on those who come to it to perfect their education, the proper thing to do would be to isolate and define what Jules Romains would call *"l'âme unanime"* of each college; thus one could show what an American gains, or loses, by becoming a Harvard man or a Princeton man, and whether the seal with which he is marked impoverishes his personality or enriches it, as the high priest of *l'unanimisme* would have it. "I want to go to Princeton," says the hero of *This Side of Paradise,* one of the most famous of the university novels. "I don't know why, but I think of all Harvard men as sissies, like I used to be, and all Yale men as wearing big blue sweaters and smoking pipes."[2] The idea is there, but things are not so simple, and it would take an analyst of considerable subtlety to get to the bottom of these imponderables.

If we pass from the general to the particular, we encounter another obstacle. The diverse groups that make up a college do not know each other very well. However intimate professors and students may be, the latter never manage to learn—fortunately—what goes on among the faculty. At least this is true in regard to professional matters, for the students do sometimes chance to catch an adequate glimpse of the private lives of their masters. This explains how the best satire on professors and their wives happens to be in *The Professor's Wife*, written by Bravig Imbs in 1928 upon his leaving Dartmouth College.[3] If, in general, the students have only a very vague idea of the mentality of the teachers, the latter, in their turn, see only the most respectable aspect of student life. They have tendencies toward idealism, and most of them would be quite surprised if they could peek at the scenes that take place in the shadows of the parks or behind the closed windows of the beautiful buildings garlanded with ivy. Moreover, if they saw these things, they most likely would not be able to make use of them. Prudence is all the brake needed to stop professors from obeying their feeble impulses to write.

In 1931 when John Uhler published *Cane Juice* he was asked to resign.

Not all the truth is safe to tell, even under democratic systems where the citizens make a point of being free. And because he described the dissoluteness of certain young women at Louisiana State University in rather vivid, but not at all exaggerated, pages, J. E. Uhler was called a slanderer by the ecclesiastic

---

[2] F. Scott Fitzgerald, *This Side of Paradise* (New York: Charles Scribner's Sons, 1920), p. 27.

[3] George Stewart, in *Doctor's Oral* (1939), has described with merciless exactitude a group of professors acting as an examination committee. M.E.C.

F. J. Gassler, champion of the fair sex. In *Passions Spin the Plot* (1934), Vardis Fisher, an English professor at Montana State University wrote in a prefatory passage: "I may be fired before another year is out. But what of it? Better men than I have been kicked out and greater men than I have starved for it. I won't be a Judas with my students. I won't be a hypocrite to get promotion here. I won't yield an inch beyond what I think is courageous and right."[4]

Supposing the young writer had sufficiently acute powers of analysis to dissect all segments of the university, he would find himself greatly hampered by problems of technique. How, without making errors, could he depict life in such complexity? I will be told that John Dos Passos in *Manhattan Transfer* has succeeded in making the city of New York swarm with life, in extracting its soul, in painting its infinite variety through judiciously chosen characters that are very lifelike. But when he succeeded with this tour de force, Dos Passos was no longer a beginner. He had already gotten his hand in with *One Man's Initiation, Streets of Night,* and *Three Soldiers.* But it is just after finishing college that the apprentice novelist feels an urge to explore college customs. And, at least until recent years, the curricula have scarcely provided any resources for the future men of letters.

Consequently, no satisfactory study of college life in its entirety has yet been written. George Weller attempted to write one in *Not to Eat, Not for Love* (1933). This is a heavy and confused work which wears the reader out. The atmosphere of Harvard (where the author was graduated in 1929) does not come through.[5] George Weller was unable to cut and prune and

---

[4] Vardis Fisher, *Passions Spin the Plot* (New York: Doubleday, Doran & Co., 1934), p. 11.

[5] Other novelized studies of life at Harvard can be found in the works of Charles Macomb Flandrau (*Harvard Episodes,* 1897; *The Diary of a Freshman,* 1931; *Sophomores Abroad,* 1935); in *They Still Say No* (1939), by Wells Lewis, son of Sinclair Lewis; *Colonel of the Crimson,* by Robert S. Playfair (1940); and *Grand Crossing,* the first novel of Alexander Saxton (1943). M.E.C.

thereby open perspectives in the dense mass of documents and observations that he had accumulated. The result is an indigestible, overly refined novel which does not always escape the charge of pedantry. The general spirit of it is indicated by the choice of the title, taken from the following passage of Emerson:

Went yesterday to Cambridge and spent most of the day at Mount Auburn; got my luncheon at Fresh Pond, and went back again to the woods. After much wandering and seeing many things, four snakes gliding up and down a hollow for no purpose that I could see—not to eat, not for love, but only gliding. . . .[6]

In 1937 Millie Hite Moody undertook, in *Towers With Ivy,* to show us a college not only in space but also in time. She follows the evolution of a college from 1835 to 1933 and is content to indicate the changing manners by the usual methods —description of dress and contrasts between the work and play of earlier times and their counterparts today. Those who are interested in such retrospective studies will do better to follow the adventures of Jerry Grant in *This Was Life,* by James Weber Linn (1936). There they will see what one did at the University of Chicago at the end of the last century.

More modest in their ambitions, the majority of the young authors prefer to describe themselves in a university setting; hence, as temperaments vary, we have an autobiographical novel that is languid, cynical, or rebellious. This is why these books are worth the attention of anyone attempting to follow the evolution of American society. They are like period specimens; for the authors, being by the mere fact of their youth sensitive to the influences of the day, put on precisely, as did Peau d'Ane,[7] the robes that show the colors of the times. This is to say that they quickly begin to seem somewhat dated, and many of them give the reader an impression comparable to that

---

[6] *Journals of Ralph Waldo Emerson,* ed. Edward Waldo Emerson and Waldo Emerson Forbes, III (Boston, 1910), p. 270.

[7] Princess wearing an ass's skin in Charles Perrault's story "Peau d'Ane."

given by the early works of Larbaud or Morand. No one writes that kind of thing any more: the 1920s and the old *mal du siècle* all over again; the postwar period with its "drifting" individuals that Phillippe Soupault tells us about; in America, prohibition and intensive emancipations to the encroaching rhythms of jazz. Of that age—which he had baptized the "Jazz Age"—Scott Fitzgerald is the best representative. He was its faithful mirror in his collections of short stories, *Flappers and Philosophers* (1921) and *Tales of the Jazz Age* (1922), and in his novels, *This Side of Paradise* (1920), *The Beautiful and Damned* (1922), and *The Great Gatsby* (1925). After *All the Sad Young Men* (1926), with its very revealing title, Fitzgerald disappeared from the world of letters. The cosmopolites of Montparnasse led him from bar to bar. That is the surest method of suicide for writers who feel impotence coming on. The rapid disintegration of such uprooted talents is the most powerful argument that the disciples of Barrès could oppose to M. André Gide. As soon as he is outside his borders, the American starts to crumble. An apparently robust plant, he does not withstand transplantation. In 1934 Scott Fitzgerald had a brief reawakening. He published *Tender Is the Night,* which has a fine title, taken from Keats' "Ode to a Nightingale," but is a miscarried novel. One feels in it a touching effort to be up to date. In 1934 (alas!) the young people were no longer so sad and the "Jazz Age" was toning down. Scott Fitzgerald could sing only one kind of music. *Tender Is the Night* is a terrible false note.

This Side of Paradise, for which Rupert Brooke furnished the title, remains, along with *The Great Gatsby,* one of the most significant documents of the first postwar years. It is the dance of Amory Blaine in front of successive mirrors: Beatrice, his mother; Princeton with its gothic towers; and all the chosen maidens—Isabelle, Clara, Rosalind, and Eleanor. College, religion, women—everything is disillusioning to this languishing idealist who finds refuge only in bars.

It is interesting to compare this 1923 type of youth with the

1938 type as described by Jack Iams in *Nowhere With Music*. Here again, in the first third of the book, the setting is Princeton. A conservative Princeton is seen through the heated brain of a young radical, John Everett. Every bit as romantic as Amory Blaine, John Everett is a rebel on principle. He likes to be talked about, and after breaking all the rules of the college (rules which at most are valid for the middle class) , he proudly gets himself expelled. Instead of languishing in moonlight reveries, he joins the Communist party. As a companion for this youth who is so representative of 1938, the author has provided a woman who is no less so: she is the most shameless specimen of American womanhood. She is a liberated woman, who marries an honest fool for his money and abandons him one night to run off to Europe with John Everett and her grandfather, an old drunkard. The militant Communist has become a militant gigolo and finds this new occupation more remunerative and more exhilarating. As for the woman, Nina, after growing indignant over her husband's suit for divorce, something she learned about upon returning to Chicago with the body of her grandfather, she embarks again, this time for the Balearic Islands, where the revolution catches her with John among a small group of eccentrics who have come to Palma to warm their sloth in the sun. *Nowhere With Music* is a cynical and brutal novel, yet very remarkable for a first book, and not in the least false, for the John Everetts tend to multiply today in the colleges, where one can achieve notoriety more quickly by violating the most elementary principles of propriety and dignity than by conforming to the rules of life that are sullied, in the eyes of these unbridled young people, by the inherent blemishes of the capitalistic system.

Between these two extreme types, one could arrange a complete scale of novels. In the area of the romantic tear-jerker, one of the most significant is *Spirals,* by Aaron Marc Stein (1930) . Because the author, who is Jewish, suffered from the ostracism, relative though it was, of which he believed himself to be the victim at Princeton, he analyzes, in a very annoying, telegraphic style, a case of the inferiority complex that is usual among the young people of his race. If we transfer this voluntary martyr to *The Sun Also Rises,* by Ernest Hemingway (1926), we will have the character of Robert Cohn, about whom Hemingway tells us at the beginning: "He cared nothing for boxing, in fact he disliked it, but he learned it painfully and thoroughly to counteract the feeling of inferiority and shyness he had felt on being treated as a Jew at Princeton." The hero of *Spirals* does not even learn to box. He is content to wail, and the hypertrophy of his ego is such that the university life shrinks to a simple background whose insignificance hardly explains the suffering which he accuses it of inflicting.

On the side of aggressive romanticism one must read *Passions Spin the Plot* (1934), the second part of a tetralogy that Vardis Fisher has devoted to Vridar Hunter. Vridar is a feverish youth, the brother of Thomas Wolfe's heroes, who is driven by all the furies and demons that hell possesses. The first volume of the series, *In Tragic Life* (1932), traces forcefully and colorfully the agonies of Vridar when, as a child, he encounters lies, cruelty, death, and the whole range of human misery. New disillusionments await him when he arrives at the university.

And he strove for a long while to believe that college was what he had imagined it would be. He tried to keep his faith and his dream. He resisted the truth of what he saw and fought stubbornly against it. But the evidence of his folly was overwhelming and little by little, in spite of all he could do, it filled him with dismay. Week after week, month after month, he saw more clearly that Wasatch College was a noisy melodrama, a grotesque assortment of postures, a stupendous farce. Its disregard of truth appalled him. Its fawning obeisance to wealth and politics made him sick.[8]

And at the beginning of the novel, the author, speaking in his own right, says:

[8] *Passions Spin the Plot,* p. 76.

For I remember when I first entered this college as a student, with my heart out of me at the wonder of it; and how I sat in awe before my instructors; and how my hunger for honest and fearless leadership was greater than my hunger for bread. A few students come here with the credulity that I had and they find, not wisdom and courage, but meanness and envy and feuds. There's more than one kind of murder, and the worst kind, in my opinion, is to be found in our universities.[9]

We would like to have some proof of all this, but Vardis Fisher is too preoccupied with his neurotic hero to give us any that is convincing. He does no more than make him evolve in a strictly limited set of vicious friends and easy women who shock his false modesty. Thenceforth Vridar appears only as an uninteresting booby who, had he made a better choice of friends, would have formed an entirely different opinion of the college. To present things through the brain of a blundering neurotic among a few black sheep is to run the risk of painting some very inaccurate pictures of a world where one can see as much good as bad when one does not put on blinders beforehand.

The same pessimistic thesis is found in *Against the Wall* (1929), by Kathleen Millay, sister of the poet Edna St. Vincent Millay. The work is not without merit, even though the author purposes much less to analyze the manners of the young women who study at Vassar than to point out the faults of that institution. She censures especially the curriculum, the standardization of ideas, and the aristocratic spirit which, according to her, reigns over that very famous college. "It was only a place for girls whose wealthy parents wanted a diploma to exhibit to the world. Or wanted not to be bothered for four nice carefree years. It was no place for a student, that was sure."[10] Miss Millay scarcely illustrates her protests. She barely sketches a few scenes of everyday life. She prefers interior monologues and the sonorous flow of images—a favorite technique of the surrealists—which enable her to advance her thesis. It is always easier to make characters argue than to make them live.

[9] *Ibid.*, p. 11.
[10] *Against the Wall* (New York: Macaulay, 1929), p. 412.

Vassar is also taken to task in *Consider the Daisies,* by Gertrude Carrick (1941), whereas Smith College finds an affectionate interpreter in Marian G. Champagne, author of *The Cauliflower Heart* (1944). On the other hand, June Wetherell, in *But That Was Yesterday* (1943), hurls at the women's colleges all the invectives she knows.

The antithesis of these arrogantly pretentious novels is to be found in the works of the authors who, disdaining the question of studies, see only the frivolous aspects of college. In 1924 *The Plastic Age,* by Percy Marks, had a great vogue because of some scenes of small orgies which were very daring at that time. *Unforbidden Fruit,* by Warner Fabian (1928), goes much farther, for it deals only with the culpable diversions of three students, Starr Mowbray, Sylvia Hartnett, and Verity Clark, nicknamed "the three H.B.V.'s" (hard-boiled virgins). According to W. Fabian, the problems of sexual life would seem to be the only preoccupation in the women's colleges, an opinion that is undermined by its excessiveness, even though one cannot deny that this kind of H.B.V. exists in all the American educational centers, and in numbers greater than three.

The demon of concupiscence, even when it is not the only reason for a novel to be written, always has some kind of place in the accounts of university life. It is this demon who grimaces behind Gene Davidson, hero of *Young Gentlemen Rise,* by Travis Ingham (1935). Gene made his acquaintance in preparatory school through a book entitled *Sexual Life of the Child.* And during the four years he spends at Yale he escapes the demon's snares, not by scorning him as Saint Theresa did, but by intensive participation in athletics. Not until his senior year has passed does he regain serenity thanks to an obliging girl who gives him certain encouragements that his nature asks only to hear.

Trio, by Dorothy Baker (1943), and *The Folded Leaf,* by William Maxwell (1945), deserve a special place. Mrs. Baker attracted attention in 1938 through her novel with the unfortunate title, *Young Man With a Horn.* It was not, as one might

184 THE AMERICAN COLLEGE NOVEL

believe, the study of a young cuckold, but the story of a young trumpet player.[11] *Trio,* a much more somber work, is based on the hold that Pauline Maury, a French woman teaching in a women's college, exercises over one of her students. This cursed woman naturally comes into conflict with Ray Mackenzie, who loves the victim and tries to release her from the grip of a spell which he knows to be Sapphic in nature. Thence develops a very moving drama against a background of university life that has been carefully studied and fairly presented.[12]

The Folded Leaf presents college life through two adolescents, Spud and Lymie, who are linked by a friendship that borders on love. Neither one suspects the truth. They are at the age of moral as well as psychological uncertainty. A young woman causes them to break up, for they both fall in love with her, or at least think they do. An attempt at suicide ends this excellent and extremely subtle novel, which is admirable for its close observation. Around the two heroes evolve a whole group of students, both men and women, as well as several types of professors. There is no exaggeration, no biased intent. *The Folded Leaf* seems to me the most exact picture yet painted of the principal aspects of university life in the United States. The value of the psychological study which forms its basis shows that William Maxwell is remarkably equipped for analytical writing, a quality which is as noticeable as it is rare in a country where there is less interest in man than in his vain fancies.

In American colleges the fires of alcohol always glow more brightly than those of lust. The reason is that many still regard the pleasures of the flesh as sin *par excellence,* with a significance that is augmented by an old background of puritanism.

---

[11] Of course, to the English-speaking public the title is not in the least unfortunate, since the horns of a cuckold always come in pairs.

[12] *Trio* was adapted for the stage by Dorothy and Howard Baker. Banned at first by producers, the play (three acts and four scenes) finally reached Broadway in December, 1944.

Information on sexual life in American colleges can be found in *Youth and Sex* (1938), by Dorothy Dunbar Bromley and Florence Haxton Britten. M.E.C.

Alcohol, on the contrary, brings prestige. No stigma whatever is attached to it. One will see its clamorous joys in all the university novels, particularly in *Boojum,* by Charles Wertenbaker (1928), who borrowed the title from Lewis Carroll, the "boojums" being the total of our unexpressed desires. The setting is the University of Virginia, where it has always been a point of honor to drink spirits neat. Driven by an obscure need for escape, the hero, Stuart Lee Breckenbridge, flees either into the artificial paradise that gin and whiskey procure for him, or into the great world where the most picaresque adventures await him.

Since the American is neither caustic nor spiteful by nature, the *roman à clef* is the exception. The best one is *The Professor's Wife,* by Bravig Imbs, in which the faculty of Dartmouth, the great college of New Hampshire, is pitilessly ridiculed. This book was written in Paris, at the instigation of Elliot Paul, and published on the recommendation of Bernard Fay. Its publication caused, at least in the small town of Hanover where Dartmouth is located, a stir similar to that created in the beginning of the century in the port of Toulon by the release of *Les Maritimes,* by Olivier Sailor. "Little by little," Bravig Imbs wrote, "I received word from America about the book's success: the critics were very kindly disposed, mostly because it was the first book to come out of Paris that was not morbid or melancholy, and to my delight, it was censored in the State of New Hampshire. Dartmouth students had only to cross the river to be in Vermont and the long winter evenings in Hanover were considerably shortened that year, I understand, the students gathering in groups to read aloud from the book, thus making the time fly."[13] *The Professor's Wife* is very amusing even for the reader who does not know the originals of the characters, for Bravig Imbs has selected his victims from types so widespread in American university milieux that one

[13] *Confessions of Another Young Man* (New York: Henkle-Yewdale House, 1936), p. 249.

could find replicas of them in all the colleges. The heroine, Delia Ramson, dominates in all her Molièresque grandeur the other *précieuses ridicules* who, because they are professors' wives, pride themselves on their fashionable gatherings where their pretentious nonsense, allied with their snobbery, can expand freely. ("I have just read your book," Blaise Cendrars said to the author. "Seigneur! what a woman! what a woman!"[14]) There are also the amateur musicians, the aesthete fresh from Oxford, and the old hypocrite who, having caroused all summer in Paris, makes edifying speeches to put young people on guard against the perversities of old Europe—a whole burlesque and harmless fauna which today would have to include the young Communist professor, newly returned from Russia, to whom the fashionably radical women listen with their mouths open and their eyes softened by pardisiac visions.

The excellent beginning in stinging satire had, alas, no sequel. Installed in Paris, where for a while he worked for an American newspaper, Bravig Imbs rapidly went to pieces in the mephitic atmosphere of Montparnasse. He made the mistake of

[14] *Ibid.* For a long time the model for this portrait, the wife of a professor of English, remained unaware of the book. Her friends, fearing that if she recognized herself in *The Professor's Wife* she would change from eccentric to completely mad, managed to keep the book out of her way. It is this incident in the academic life of Dartmouth to which M. André Maurois alludes in *La Machine à lire les pensées:* "A Westmouth graduate with a brilliant and rebellious mind, having become a fashionable novelist after his college years, got the idea of using Mrs. Philipps as the central character in one of his books and drew a portrait that resembled her too much. The first member of the college group to receive the novel could not help feeling pity when he imagined the painful effect it would have on Mrs. Philipps if she read this cruel text. He immediately alerted his colleagues and a real conspiracy developed to keep the book away from any place where the Philippses might come upon it. All the copies in the local bookstore were bought. The library copy, miraculously, was always being read, as were the journals that contained reviews of the book. To avoid any surprise, everyone swore never to speak of it." Pp. 122–23. M.E.C.

straying into the entourage of Gertrude Stein. The Ogress of the rue de Fleurus swallowed him whole. In the last pages of *The Autobiography of Alice B. Toklas* she depicts him as a young man who was eager to please and who could play the violin to Elliot Paul's accordion. Two books that he wrote with difficulty were rejected by all the American publishers. One of them, *Chatterton,* was published in a French translation by the Baroness Sellière; the other, *The Cats,* was published in Dutch. Not until 1936 did we have the *Confessions of Another Young Man,* a pathetic avowal of impotence but an important document for the study of bohemia in Montparnasse. Bitterness in it sometimes takes the place of the trenchant verve which constituted the charm of *The Professor's Wife,* but here and there one again finds silhouettes that are well cut out and jabs that, though apparently innocuous, find their mark. Witness the last lines of the volume on the subject of Gertrude Stein and her salon:

It was amazing how rapidly the little court was dispersed. All the devoted admirers had become exiles, more or less chagrined. All the friends of the devoted admirers had left the salon as well, out of sympathy, and the rue de Fleurus must have seemed a desolate, deserted spot for a while. No more parties, no more teas, no more hours of gossip, no more recriminating against a common fate with publishers, no more dropping in after dinner, no more little cakes, no more exciting painter discoveries to discuss, no more manuscripts to criticize, no more voyages in the country,—no more anything, but memories. . . .
Even now, sometimes, I still regret the little cakes.[15]

There is no such acidulous humor in another *roman à clef,* David McCloud's *Dance Out the Answer* (1932), which takes its title from Shakespeare. It is a heavy novel which does not move forward and is uninteresting except to readers who are familiar with the manners and customs of Hamilton College.

---

[15] *Confessions of Another Young Man,* pp. 300–301.

These readers can recognize the dean, the young professor who shows an excessive interest in his students, and a certain person of note who is very much in view on the literary scene in New York and who undoubtedly would have preferred that David McCloud had forgotten his existence.[16]

One curious book should be set apart as unique, Mary Jane Ware's *The Tree Has Roots* (1937), an account of university life as it is seen by the employees—gardeners, sweepers, restaurant managers, building inspectors, and typists. The idea was ingenious and could have given birth to a study of the keenest interest. Unfortunately the talent of the author was not equal to the task, and the result is disappointing, to say the least.

Her Soul to Keep, by Ethel Cook Eliot (1935), and *It Began in Eden,* by Frances Shelley Wees (1936), are two sufficient examples of novels which are situated in university towns but have nothing to do with college life (or very little). The first is a thesis novel in which questions of sin and illegitimate birth are presented from the Catholic point of view; the second is a trite love story.

Finally, it is possible for a campus regulation to serve as a pretext for a work of imagination. Edward Hope, recalling that at Princeton women are not allowed in the students' rooms after 6 P.M., wrote a burlesque novel, *She Loves Me Not* (1933), in which a dancer named Curly, fleeing from gangsters and from the police who accuse her of a crime which she did not commit, takes refuge in a dormitory during the prohibited hours and consequently sets off a series of preposterous adventures.[17]

We are touching the realm of the crime novel. The important

---

[16] In *Beer for the Kitten* (1939), Hester Pine satirizes the professors of Union College. The faculty and administration are scarcely treated any better in *Geese in the Forum,* by Lawrence Edward Watkins (1940). *The Hunted,* by Albert J. Guérard (1944), pitilessly exposes the cruelty of university women. *These Bars of Flesh,* by T. S. Stribling (1938), contains a broad caricature of the summer courses offered by a college in the South. M.E.C.

[17] The only interesting thing about this very mediocre novel is that it provided the basis for a rather funny light comedy which ran for several months in New York in 1934. M.E.C.

role played by colleges in American life is sufficient to explain why a detective writer gladly selects college campuses and buildings to perpetrate his heinous crimes. *Smell the Dead,* by Carey Magoon (1943), and *Scandal Has Two Faces,* by Mary E. Campbell (1944), are two recent cases in point.[18] There is another one which I shall not allow myself to overlook, since I am in a sense its godfather. It is *The Widening Stain,* by W. Bolingbroke Johnson (1942), otherwise known as Morris Bishop. Mr. Morris Bishop, a professor at Cornell University, having written in 1940 a book on Ronsard that was fatuous enough to make the stones weep, took it ill that I reviewed the book with the severity it deserved. *The Widening Stain* was his vengeance. Having transformed me into Lucie Coindreau, a female professor of French and a great eater of garlic, one fine day he made me topple over the banisters of a gallery in the college library, where my corpse was found the next day with the head in a pool of blood. That death caused me very little suffering; but the reputation of W. Bolingbroke Johnson gained nothing by it, for many readers identified him with one of his characters, Professor Parry, a dolt who mistakes himself for a wit and writes limericks as lamentably insipid as certain trifling poems published in the *New Yorker* for which, it would seem, Morris Bishop is responsible.

It is clear from this rapid survey that the great synthesizing novel remains to be written.[19] Most of the works we have pointed out are more or less malevolent (to that extent they resemble

---

[18] One could cite also *Harvard Has a Homicide,* by Timothy Fuller (1936), and *Dear Dead Professor,* by K. Alison La Roche (1945). M.E.C.

[19] I have intentionally omitted the numerous novels in which college life figures incidentally. Princeton figures thus in *Those Hitch-hikers,* by Booth Jameson (1930), *The Leaf Is Green,* by John V. Craven (1931), *This Our Exile,* by David Burnham (1931), *Dawn Breaks the Heart,* by William Davey (1941), and a volume of short stories, *In Princeton Town,* by Day Edgar (1929). Harvard has a role in *The Sound and the Fury,* by William Faulkner (1929), and in *Of Time and the River,* by Thomas Wolfe (1935), etc. M.E.C.

the French military novels, whether the example be *Cavalier Miserey, Sous-Offs,* or *Gaietés de l'Escadron*). They were written by misfits, rebels, or neurasthenics—in short, by malcontents. They completely ignore the admirable side of American university life: the conscientious and devoted professors, the steady toilers whose lights burn into the wee hours, the excellent libraries where some first-rate work is done, the happy and healthy life of hundreds of young people who combine work and sports and pleasure in complete honesty and forthrightness, having no more malice than good healthy animals would have, and the durable friendships which develop and which are confirmed each year at the various class reunions around commencement time. But that is a side which is all the more difficult to present because the students themselves do not take it into account. We are poor judges of what we see at too close range. We remember the bad days and forget the happy ones. Moreover, in regard to college life, distance is not without its dangers. Nothing lends itself to idealization more than the years of adolescence, and the picture that a mature man forms of his university, softened as it is by the memories of vanished youth, is liable to be as partial and as deformed as the view which the newly released student can have of it. Ill-feelings having disappeared, nothing remains but an idyllic tableau that is tame and devoid of charm.

What young Americans need most is a reasonable dose of skepticism and cynicism. Spoiled by idealism, they experience, if they are intelligent, the bitterness that disillusionment brings. They are amazed to find in a university, which after all is no more than a microcosm, the things that one finds throughout the world: intrigue, pettiness, hypocrisy, and stupidity. They seem not to suspect that these are vices inherent in human nature, and so they get on their high horses. Around the age of twenty, one is pleased to feel that he has the soul of a knight errant. The day when the future writer enters college free of puerile illusions which keep him in constant danger of mistaking the moon for green cheese; the day when, inclined toward pessimism, he remembers Voltaire's remark that there is no evil from which some good does not come; the day when, disposed to reform the world, he listens to Montaigne whisper in his ear, "What do I know?" that day, armed with the balancing pole which is the correct view of man with his flaws and his greatness, he will be able, without too much danger, to accomplish that dance on the tightrope which is the elaboration of a realistic novel without extremes and with complete equity. If the basis is solid, one will forgive him for the false steps that he might take, for the clumsiness of a first performance could do little harm to a narrative of indisputable authenticity.

COLLEGE LIFE

AND THE AMERICAN NOVEL

PART TWO: 1945–1964 *

Even more than of her automobiles, her bathrooms and her kitchens, America is proud of her colleges and universities. She would gladly say, as Gargantua wrote to his son, "The world is full of learned men, erudite teachers, and huge libraries; I do not believe the ages of Plato, Cicero or Papinian afforded such facilities for study as we have today. From now on it is unthinkable to appear in public or in polite company without having been turned to a high polish in the workshop of Minerva." Among the Americans that workshop takes various forms, all of them sumptuous. All styles are represented from Greek temples to rabbit hutches of glass and reinforced concrete, with a little Roman and great deal of Gothic to link it all together. I even know a university where the architect who designed the theater took his inspiration from the papal palace in Avignon. Since it is imperative for young Americans "to take their places in society" as early as possible, at the end of September they regretfully abandon the mountains and beaches or take boats and planes by assault in order to return from the four corners of the earth at the appointed time to the *alma mater*

* In an earlier form this article appeared as "La Vie de collège dans le roman américain," in *Arts* (November 13, 1963). Reprinted by permission of Gallimard. Translation by G.M.R.

whose doors have been opened to them by entrance examinations. And they spend four years in this singular kind of paradise; for, instead of lilies and other symbols of purity, one scarcely sees anything bloom there except a full complement of mortal sins along with numerous venial sins for good measure.

At least this is the conclusion one is forced to reach after reading the current crop of novels about college life. One had to reach that same conclusion before the Second World War, but in that faraway time the young writers rebelled upon contact with a reality that was very different from what the silly dithyrambs of parents faithful to their *alma mater* had led them to expect. They wrote anti-university novels just as France's young writers, barely out of their regiments, wrote anti-military novels at the end of the nineteenth century.

Today the tone has changed. The writers take things philosophically, when they are not openly amusing themselves. The changing mores and the frankness in narration and expression permit them to depict many scenes of college life, barely touched on in former times, in colors that are all the more vivid because the authors, generally very young, would believe they were betraying the liberation of their generation if they did not show themselves to be as shameless as monkeys. In other words, the novel of college life has become pornographic. But it did not do so overnight.

As formerly, in the center of these books one finds the author in the role of amused actor and spectator, in keeping with the usual practice in first novels. It is customary not to mention the name of the college, but with perfidious hypocrisy the publisher never fails, in the blurb on the jacket, to tell the reader where the author studied. Thus we know, for example, that since Scott Sullivan was graduated from Yale in 1958, the university that provides the setting for *The Shortest and Gladdest Years* (1962) is not Harvard or Princeton or Columbia. If I begin with this novel, selected from the many that have appeared in recent years, the reason is that, in my opinion, it gives us the most accurate and above all the most complete picture of student life in the United States. It has a very simple structure and a meaningful title. It is not slow or boring to read. Through four comrades, each one of whom narrates one of the four sections of the book, we watch four years of college go by— student years, but of study the author says almost nothing. At long intervals there is the matter of a paper to be thrown together as quickly as possible. As examinations approach, the student takes a few books, some notes, and a transistor radio to the beach. There, beside the coed he is dating for the day, he "studies." It is not that these young people have been idle all year. One of them in particular is busy day and night, sustained by quantities of whiskey, with the university newspaper. The training is excellent if he wishes to launch a career in journalism later. Then too the arrangements for weekends take a great deal of time. The students cannot stay in one place. They go to New York or to the mountains for skiing or to the nearby women's colleges, for though they have neither the time nor the desire for love, they nevertheless gratify their sexual pangs every time they have a chance. For this kind of activity the football Saturdays are especially propitious.

In *Entry E,* by Richard Frede (1958), another Yale graduate, we find a two-hundred-page account of one of these athletic weekends. The *pièce de résistance* in this novel is what is called in college argot a "gang bang" (called also a "gang shay" or a "gang shag"). Some male students take a girl, usually one of easy virtue (but sometimes also of excellent family), into their room, get her drunk, and invite their friends. And each one takes his turn with her. First come, first served, as in a barber-shop. In the hall one boy stands guard at the door to keep the gate-crashers out. In *Entry E* Richard Frede, feeling pity for the victim, sends her a Sir Galahad who rescues her from her clients, sobers her up as best he can, and escorts her back to the station, repentant but ready to begin all over again.

If gang bangs are part of the autumn entertainment, panty

raids usually take place in the spring, when the sap rises. There is a description of this activity in Herbert Kubly's *The Whistling Zone* (1963), which is set in a western university, although the tradition is spread throughout the territory of the Union. The panty raid makes a pleasurable combination of the infantry charge and the striptease. On a spring evening the students form a raucous group and set out to storm a girls' dormitory. They are rarely able to enter, for the doors are guarded by ferocious Cerberuses. That being the case, the captive Sabines appear at their windows and throw panties, brassieres, and other small objects to their frustrated ravishers, to keep them in the desirable state of mind until the next weekend, when the girls will return the visit. Similarly, in the Middle Ages, ladies high in their towers dropped flowers and ribbons to their champions. Those were the barbarous Dark Ages. Happily we have changed all that.

Among the most recent of these joyous novels of erotic and alcoholic adventures, I will mention only two, written by young Californians: *What Can You Do,* by James Leigh (1965), now a professor at San Francisco State College; and *The Sterile Cuckoo,* by John Nichols (1965), who studied at Hamilton College. In them we find the same type of adventures, notably some rather incredible debauches in the student clubs called fraternities.

These various modes of merrymaking are pleasures of the campus. But there are also places reserved especially for the longer holidays. The most famous of those for a long time was Fort Lauderdale, Florida. It was estimated that twenty thousand students of both sexes went there to frolic in the spring. We are indebted to Professor Glendon Swarthout for our knowledge of what went on there. Already known for a very good novel, *They Came to Cordura,* Glendon Swarthout published in 1961 *Where the Boys Are,* a well-handled, lively, and very funny story. It is all told by a coed from the Midwest, an ingenuous libertine who has never seen the sea or boats or palm trees but who knows that Fort Lauderdale is "where the boys are." In fact they are there by the thousands, and they make their presence known. I doubt that ancient Rome ever saw such Bacchanalias. I had the opportunity of seeing the film based on this novel in the company of one of my students who himself had gone one Easter to celebrate the Resurrection in this sunny brothel. "Don't think for a minute that this film is exaggerated," he said. "Actually it doesn't go far enough." That is when I began to take Glendon Swarthout's book seriously, however unlikely the events in it may seem. After what the student said, it is easy to understand why the inhabitants of the region, after earning extra money during the college vacation periods for several years, eventually drove these undesirable tourists away. The vogue of Fort Lauderdale ended in 1961, and then it was Daytona Beach which was privileged to receive the assault wave of this intellectual and cultivated youth, a wave which, according to one motel owner, equalled the arrival of four divisions of marines.[1]

What is the situation among the young women? Are their famous colleges dealt with any more kindly than those of the boys? Unfortunately not, if we judge by the novels of recent years. Smith College, which in 1944 was treated sympathetically by Marian Champagne in *The Cauliflower Heart,* found a less indulgent interpreter in Nora Johnson. The heroine of *A Step Beyond Innocence* (1961), Sally Fraits, prefers to search for a man rather than to search for knowledge in the library. Her excuse is that she wishes to know what love really is. No doubt her intellect is not very keen, for she takes a long time to find the answer; meanwhile, the multiplication of her experience becomes the goal of her life. Vassar College, taken to task in 1929 by Kathleen Millay in *Against the Wall,* and again in 1941 by Gertrude Garrick in *Consider the Daisies,* brooked a new

---

[1] The excellent reporter Sanche de Grammont devoted three articles to these rites of spring in the *New York Herald Tribune,* March 29–31, 1964. M.E.C.

outrage when Mary McCarthy published *The Group,* to which
I shall return. All these novels are studies of manners tending,
through the exposition of a few ideas here and there, toward the
thesis novel. But sometimes they present psychological cases of
a type more rare in men's colleges than in women's.

I am thinking especially of two books which deal with the
powerful influence which a woman, a professor in one instance
and a visiting lecturer in the other, can acquire, sometimes
without knowing it, over her students. This is the subject of
Trio, by Dorothy Baker (1943), and of *Give Me Myself,* by
Susan Sherman (1961), the story of Nona Greene's passionate admiration for Evelyn Gordon McKenna, an Irishwoman teaching in the summer school where Nona is completing her
studies. From the very first lecture Nona catches fire—"crys-
tallizes," Stendhal would say—and deifies this woman who,
beneath her brilliant academic finish, is nothing but an alcoholic given to orgies. In the final pages Nona finds her idol in
Florence dead drunk in a slum, lying in the filth of a hole-in-the-
floor toilet which, with the aid of a cot, has been transformed
into her bedroom. Nona, out of funds, is repatriated by her
consul and returns to the fold seeing herself clearly at last after
this expedition into the forbidden regions. The author was
twenty years old when she wrote this very somber story, the most
brutal illustration of the theme common to these novels of
restless adolescence, a kind of race toward destruction fueled
with alcohol and eroticism, in the hope that the heroine, after
going astray, can regain "her right mind at last." On the masculine side, problems of abnormal psychology appear particularly in the novels describing life in the "prep schools" (for
example, John Burns's *Lucifer With a Book,* published in 1949,
with a very meaningful title) or in the military schools such as
The Citadel, of which Calder Willingham draws an extremely
disquieting picture in *End As a Man* (1947), or Gordon
Military Adademy, called Mason Military Academy in *The
Terrible Swift Sword,* by Arthur Steuer (1956). In the latter, the

theft of a revolver allows the sadistic guardians to indulge in all their charming tricks.

The novels by professors who have been in close contact with college administration and with the machinations regarding faculty promotions offer—in addition to the inevitable constants, alcohol and sex—some new elements: ambition, jealousy, toadying, backbiting and calumny. Some of these books have become classics: for example, *Purely Academic* (1958), by Stringfellow Barr, who must know what he is talking about since he has been not only a professor, but also president of St. John's College at Annapolis. In this novel the satire is merciless, and the hurricanes which assail the coasts of Florida each autumn are no more damaging. *Pictures from an Institution* (1954) gave the poet Randall Jarrell a chance to say his word about the so-called "progressive" schools. Here we find this lapidary phrase: "Sex, greed, envy, power, money: Gertrude knew that these were working away at Benton—though in sublimated form, sometimes—exactly as they work away everywhere else."[2] In *The Groves of Academe* (1952) Mary McCarthy had not been any more gentle toward this same kind of institution; and in *The Party at Cranton* (1960), a novel without dialogue and with only the author as speaker, the talented critic John Aldridge deals critically with the deeds and gestures of vainly pretentious characters "who, in losing passion and pain, had lost the means of human relationships."[3] I would not like to omit *Learner's Permit* (1962), which is less well known because it is more recent, but which, using a vaudeville plot, has more to say on "academe" than all the works I have just discussed. The author, Lawrence Lafore, a professor at Swarthmore, has been spoiled by the gods, who gave him almost diabolical perspicacity that is assisted by a fine sense of humor.

[2] Randall Jarrell, *Pictures from an Institution* (New York: Alfred A. Knopf, 1955), p. 106.

[3] John W. Aldridge, *The Party at Cranton* (New York: D. McKay Co., 1960), p. 16.

Pamela Hansford Johnson does not reach the high level of this masterpiece of satire in *Night and Silence, Who Is Here?* (1963), a book that is amiably funny, but nothing more.

It goes without saying that in all these novels the professors' wives receive no better treatment than their husbands. It happens even that entire novels are devoted to them, but *The Professor's Wife*, by Bravig Imbs, has never been surpassed.[4] In 1963 when John O'Hara tried in *Elizabeth Appleton* to show us a professor's wife, he succeeded only in describing the life of a small Pennsylvania town in an entirely mediocre narrative which, because of its very mediocrity, was long a leader of the best sellers.

The final question remains: what happens to the young people brought up in these institutions for which the novelists seem to have so little esteem? Mary McCarthy, with reference to Vassar, gives us in *The Group* (1963) an answer that could not be rightly generalized. The group of eight girls whose adventures she traces between a marriage and a funeral could have been a different group if she had wished. Was it for revenge on the college from which she was graduated in 1933 with all the credentials, which she still carries hung around her neck like the albatross of the Ancient Mariner? Was it that bondage which caused her to choose such unfortunate samples of the women of her country? Or was she looking for an occasion to write some smut so as to appear up-to-date, forgetting that, in order to write such things without being vulgar, one must have, as Frenchmen used to say during the era when they did not yet speak "Franglais," special graces which Heaven does not seem to have bestowed upon her? However that may be, the novel is mediocre, but significant nevertheless. In my opinion it is clearly inferior to a more recent novel which concerns boys graduated from Yale, Harvard, and Princeton—that is to say, the cream of the crop. The title of it is (no doubt in homage to William

---

[4] See Part One of this essay.

Burroughs) *The Naked Martini* (1964) and the author is John Leonard. This counterpart of *The Group* is nothing but a long series of drinking parties and fornications which begin with the interest that five boys show impetuously, each in his turn during a wild party, in a girl named Bobbie Bernstein. This is reminiscent of the mad frolics in the dormitories and fraternity houses during football weekends. After such a sparkling start the novel moves along at a great rate. The orgies follow one another in an accelerating rhythm, to the sound of Bach fugues and Mozart symphonies on the phonograph. Anyone with a diploma from a famous college must by all means demonstrate that he is cultured, and during the few minutes when the conversation is not on alcohol or sex there is always someone to drop the names of Proust or Nietzsche or to read Ezra Pound. The whole thing ends at Princeton in the most virtuous way imaginable, with a big wedding joining Bobbie Bernstein and one of the "five" named Cranston, who has had his heart set on being married at his *alma mater*. Bobbie is Jewish but Cranston is not. The two families look at each other menacingly. Bobbie saves the situation and takes revenge for the anti-Semitism that she detects by declaring to all present that in nature's good time she will have the pleasure of announcing to all her friends the birth of a future Princetonian whose paternity can be claimed by five young men. *This Side of Paradise* did not offer such a rich assortment of damaged goods, and during the conversation between Amory Blaine and his favorite girls at the foot of gothic buildings bathed in moonlight there was no chance of suddenly coming upon sentences like this one: "I always thought professors spawned nothing but neurotics. The sons were drunkards, or bohemians, or dope addicts; and the daughters were frigid, or nymphomaniacs, or manic-depressives."[5] Between 1920 and 1964 manners have changed somewhat, and today "This Side of Paradise" would be more like "This Side of Hell." Or perhaps the novelists have simply re-

[5] John Leonard, *The Naked Martini* (New York: Dial Press, 1964), p. 171.

placed teary-eyed compassion with a cynicism stripped of illusions that is more in the tone of the times.

We may ask ourselves, perhaps, why the American novelists who write of life in their colleges, to which, moreover, they themselves remain strongly attached, never mention the honest, conscientious teachers they have known or the students who work hard and still observe the fundamental rules of decency. Balzac gives us the answer in the "Preface to the *Human Comedy*," where he speaks of the "difficult literary problem which consists of making a virtuous person seem interesting." That is the whole problem. To be a novelist one must be on intimate terms with the devil. Consequently, the saints, who were sometimes great poets, were never, so far as I know, novelists. The fiend does not like edifying subjects, and anyone tempted to make use of them could not count on his aid. And besides, if one wants to live by his pen, he must write books that sell. But virtue is like crime—it does not pay. However familiar the novelists may be with the devil, none of them, neither the youthful nor the experienced, like to pull his tail. *The Group* had hardly been released when there was talk of 75,000 copies, and Hollywood was alerted. The commendable aspects of university life in the U.S.A. would never open such a gold mine.

CHECKLIST

MAURICE EDGAR COINDREAU:

A CHECKLIST

The following checklist was originally prepared by Mrs. Boyd Davis as part of a master's thesis directed by James B. Meriwether, with the full cooperation of Professor Coindreau. I am happy to acknowledge my indebtedness to all three. I have added a few titles, most of them of very recent date. Otherwise the checklist is the work of Mrs. Davis. The checklist is divided into six main categories:

A. Works translated into French from the American
B. Works translated into French from the Spanish
C. Articles
D. Reviews
E. Prefaces and Introductions
F. Miscellaneous.

Items in each category are numbered chronologically in order of publication, with the work listed first. The publisher, unless otherwise noted, is Gallimard of Paris. Unfortunately neither Mrs. Davis nor I have been able to examine all the items listed, and some of the data are incomplete. For the lacunae and all errors, I accept responsibility.

G.M.R.

A. Works translated into French from the American:

Novels and collections of stories
(Paris: Gallimard, unless otherwise noted)

1. *Manhattan Transfer*. John Dos Passos. 1928. 2 vols.

2. *L'Adieu aux armes*. Ernest Hemingway. 1932. Préface: Drieu la Rochelle.

3. *Le Soleil se lève aussi*. Ernest Hemingway. 1933. Préface: Jean Prévost.

4. *Tandis que j'agonise*. William Faulkner. 1934. Préface: Valery Larbaud.

5. *Lumière d'août*. William Faulkner. 1935. Préface: Maurice Edgar Coindreau.

6. *Le Petit Arpent du bon Dieu*. Erskine Caldwell. 1936. Préface: André Maurois.

7. *La Route au tabac*. Erskine Caldwell. 1937.

8. *Le Bruit et la fureur*. William Faulkner. 1938. Préface: Maurice Edgar Coindreau.

9. *Treize histoires*. William Faulkner. Avec R.-N. Raimbault, Ch.-P. Vorce. 1939.

10. *Des Souris et des hommes.* John Steinbeck. 1939. Préface: Joseph Kessel. Introduction: Maurice Edgar Coindreau.

11. *Un Pauvre Type.* Erskine Caldwell. 1945. Préface: Maurice Edgar Coindreau.

12. *La Feuille repliée.* William Maxwell. 1948. Préface: Maurice Edgar Coindreau.

13. *Terre tragique.* Erskine Caldwell. 1948.

14. *Les Domaines hantés.* Truman Capote. 1949. Préface: Maurice Edgar Coindreau.

15. *Les Palmiers sauvages.* William Faulkner. 1952. Préface: Maurice Edgar Coindreau.

16. *La Harpe d'herbe.* Truman Capote. 1952.

17. *Un Arbre de nuit.* Truman Capote. Avec Serge Doubrovsky. 1953.

18. *La Maison d'haleine.* William Goyen. 1954. Préface: Maurice Edgar Coindreau.

19. *Jefferson, Mississippi.* William Faulkner. Extraits: pp. 15–48; 230–48; 248–94; 294–310; 435–45; 446–58. 1956.

20. *Le Fantôme et la chair.* William Goyen. 1956. Préface: Michel Mohrt.

21. *Requiem pour une nonne.* William Faulkner. 1957. Préface: Albert Camus.

22. *La Sagesse dans le sang.* Flannery O'Connor. 1959. Préface: Maurice Edgar Coindreau.

23. *La Proie des flammes.* William Styron. 1962. Préface: Michel Butor.

24. *Les Larrons.* William Faulkner. Avec Raymond Girard. 1964. Préface: Raymond Girard.

25. *L'Hameçon d'or.* Fred Chappell. 1965.

26. *Les Noms et visages de héros.* Reynolds Price. 1965.

27. *Et ce sont les violents qui l'emportent.* Flannery O'Connor. 1965. Préface: J.M.G. Le Clézio.

28. *Feu pâle.* Vladimir Nabokov. Avec Raymond Girard. 1968.

29. *La Belle Vie.* John Dos Passos. Avec Claude Richard. Le Mercure de France, 1968.

30. *Les Confessions de Nat Turner.* William Styron. 1969.

31. *L'Arbre aux souhaits.* Wiliam Faulkner. 1969.

Short Stories

32. "Swanson et les gratte-ciel," Beverly Nichols. *La Revue nouvelle,* LVII (juin 1930), pp. 136–41.

33. "Septembre ardent," William Faulkner. *La Nouvelle revue française,* CCXX (janvier 1932), pp 49–65.

34. "Une Rose pour Emilie," William Faulkner. *Commerce,* XXIX (hiver 1932), pp. 110–37.

35. "Il Etait une reine," William Faulkner. *La Nouvelle revue française,* CCXXXIX (aout 1933), pp. 213–33.

36. "Soleil couchant," William Faulkner. *Europe,* 15 janvier 1935, pp. 37–60.

37. "L'Après-midi d'une vache," William Faulkner. *Fontaine, juin-juillet* 1943, pp. 66–81.

38. "Le Jardin des oliviers," Caroline Gordon. *Les Lettres Françaises,* Numéro 105 (29 mars 1946), p. 6ff.

39. "La Dernière porte est close," Truman Capote. *La Revue de Paris,* 55ᵉ année (décembre 1948), pp. 101–14.

40. "Deux contes," William Maxwell. *La Revue de Paris,* 55ᵉ année (février 1948), pp. 127–30.

41. "Miriam," Truman Capote. *La Revue de Paris,* 56ᵉ année (juillet 1949), pp. 109–19.

42. "Le Coq blanc," William Goyen. *La Table Ronde,* Numéro 63 (mars 1953), pp. 53–69.

43. "Le Fantôme de Raymond Emmons," William Goyen. *Figaro Littéraire,* 1 juillet 1954.

44. "Zamour," William Goyen. *La Revue de Paris,* 1955.

45. "Deux soldats," William Faulkner. *Sélections du Livre.* Paris: Gallimard, 1955, pp. 11–135.

46. "Pauv' Perrie," William Goyen. *La Nouvelle nouvelle revue française*, XLII (1 juin 1956), pp. 1032–50.

Extracts

47. *Orient Express.* John Dos Passos. *La Revue nouvelle*, XXXVI (novembre 1927), pp. 312ff.

48. "L'Homme qui disait s'appeler Jones," extrait de *1919*. John Dos Passos. *Romanciers américains.* Paris: de Noel et Steele, 1931, pp. 113–32.

49. "Meester Veelson," extrait de *1919*. John Dos Passos. *Cahiers du sud*, Tome 10, Numéro 150 (avril 1933), pp. 257–65.

50. *Lumière d'août (Fragment).* William Faulkner. *Cahiers du sud*, Tome 12, Numéro 169 (février 1935), pp. 83–101.

51. *Les Domaines hantés.* Truman Capote. *Vogue* (Edition de Paris), (mai 1949) ; *Gazette des lettres* (14 mai 1949).

52. "Les Palmiers sauvages," extrait de *Les Palmiers sauvages*. William Faulkner. *Les Temps modernes*, LXIII–LXVII (janvier–mai 1951).

53. *La Maison d'haleine.* William Goyen. *La Nouvelle nouvelle revue française*, XI (novembre 1953), pp. 769–99; XII (décembre 1953), pp. 1033–63; XIII (janvier 1954), pp. 62–95.

54. "Araignées, rats et éléphants," extrait de *Clair de lune*. Carl Sandburg. *La Revue nouvelle*, LXIII (décembre 1930), pp. 37–45.

B. Works translated into French from the Spanish:

Plays

1. "Le Patio," S. & J. Alvarez Quintero. *España*, IV (octubre–diciembre 1918), pp. 312–28.

2. "Le Chou-chou," S. & J. Alvarez Quintero. *España*, IV (octubre–diciembre 1918).

3. *Bourg-les-dames.* S. & J. Alvarez Quintero. *Cahiers du Capricorn*, no. 3. Nîmes: Jo Fabre, 1925.

4. *Divines Paroles.* Ramón del Valle-Inclán. Paris: Librairie Stock, Delamain et Boutelleau, 1927. Préface: Jean de la Nible. New edition, Gallimard, 1963. No Préface.

Fiction

5. *Jeux de Mains.* Juan Goytisolo. 1956. Préface: Maurice Edgar Coindreau.

6. *Inventions et pérégrinations d'Alfanhui.* Rafael Sánchez Ferlosio. 1957. Préface: Maurice Edgar Coindreau.

7. *Le Chemin.* Miguel Delibes. 1959.

8. *Deuil au Paradis.* Juan Goytisolo. 1959. Préface: José María Castellet.

9. *Le Masque.* Elena Quiroga. Avec Bernard Sesé. 1959. Préface: Maurice Edgar Coindreau.

10. *Fiestas.* Juan Goytisolo. 1960.

11. *Marionettes.* Ana Maria Matute. 1962.

12. *La Feuille rouge.* Miguel Delibes. 1962.

13. *Danses d'été.* Juan Goytisolo. 1964.

14. *Enfermés avec un seul jouet.* Juan Marsé. 1967.

15. *Fleur de sainteté.* Ramón del Valle-Inclán. 1967.

16. *Pièces d'identité.* Juan Goytisolo. 1968.

C. ARTICLES

In French, or on French-American Subjects
(Note: Many of Coindreau's articles from *France-Amérique* have been omitted.)

1. "Don Ramón del Valle-Inclán," *La Revue nouvelle,* XIV (septembre–octobre 1925), p. 15.

2. "Abel Hernant, ou, les Inconvénients de sourire," *La Revue nouvelle,* XV (février 1926), pp. 21–27.

3. "Le Retour des enfants prodigues—pronostique d'hiver," *La Revue du siècle,* XVI (15 novembre 1926).

4. "Sur le théâtre de Georges Kelly," *La Revue nouvelle,* XXVI (15 janvier 1927), pp. 47–53.

5. "Du côté de chez Cham," *La Revue du siècle,* XXI (15 février 1927), pp. 272–75.

6. "Manhattan et la prisonnière, ou le payement de Pots cassés," *La Revue du siècle,* XXI (1 juin 1927), pp. 226–30.

7. "Les Enfants terribles," *La Revue nouvelle,* XLIV (décembre 1928), pp. 99–104.

8. "Deux Nouveautés de Eugene O'Neill: *Strange Interlude* and *Marco Millions,*" *La Revue nouvelle,* XLII (octobre 1928), pp. 146–50.

9. "William Faulkner," *La Nouvelle revue française,* CCXXXVI (juin 1931), pp. 926–30.

10. "L'Amérique et les romans alcooliques," *Cahiers du sud,* avril 1932, pp. 166–73.

11. "Du Théâtre populaire en France de 1900 à 1925," *French Review,* VI (February 1933), pp. 181–89.

12. "Le Puritanisme de William Faulkner" [préface de *Lumière d'août*], *Cahiers du sud,* avril 1935, pp. 259–67.

13. "Hommage à Eugène Dabit," *Le Courrier des Etats-Unis,* 14 novembre 1936.

14. "Erskine Caldwell," *La Nouvelle revue française,* CCLXXVIII (1 novembre 1936), pp. 908–12.

15. "Jacques de Lacretelle de l'académie française," *Le Courrier des Etats-Unis,* 12 décembre, 16 décembre 1936.

16. "A propos des romans policiers," *Le Courrier des Etats-Unis,* 17 avril, 21 avril 1937.

17. "France and the Contemporary American Novel," *The Kansas City University Review,* III, No. 4 (1937), pp. 273–79.

18. "D'une Renaissance du roman picaresque," *Aguedal,* Numero 2 (1937), pp. 110–25.

19. "D'une chanson du Bas-Poitou que Rabelais a pu connaître," *The Romanic Review,* XXIX (April 1938), pp. 120–28.

20. "Préface pour *Le Bruit et la fureur*," *La Vie réelle*, IV (1938), pp. 83–87.

21. "La vie de collège et le roman américain," *Aguedal*, Numéro 3 (1938), pp. 195–214.

22. "Du danger des citations incomplètes," *The Romanic Review*, XXIX (December 1938), pp. 323–24.

23. "Vie et mort d'un poète," *Lettres françaises*, Numéro 4 (1942), pp. 36–46.

24. "Histoires d'alcools et de meurtres," *Les Gants du Ciel*, Numéro 4 (juin 1944), pp. 51–73.

25. "John Steinbeck," *Lettres française*, 6° année, Numéro 101 (26 avril 1946), p. 1ff.

26. "William Maxwell," *La Revue de Paris*, 55° année (février 1948), pp. 120–26.

27. "La littérature américaine contemporaine," *Larousse mensuel*, 41° année, Tome XII, Numéro 401 (janvier 1948).

28. "Une enquête américaine: le rapport Kinsey," *La Revue de Paris*, 56° année (janvier 1949), pp. 106–16.

29. "Les Prix Pulitzer," *Larousse mensuel*, 43° année, Tome XII, Numéro 429 (mai 1950).

30. "William Faulkner: prix Nobel de littérature," *France-Amérique*, CCXXXVI (26 novembre 1950), p. 9.

31. "L'Art de William Faulkner," *France-Amérique*, CCXXXVII (3 décembre 1950), pp. 9–10.

32. "William Faulkner in France," *Yale French Studies*, X (1953), pp. 85–91.

33. "Deux prix Nobel: Faulkner, Mauriac," *Bulletin de la société des professeurs français en Amérique*, janvier 1953, pp. 11–15.

34. "William Faulkner et Ernest Hemingway," *Journal de Genève*, 11 et 12 décembre 1954, p. 4.

35. "Remarques sur l'art de traduire," *France in the United States Monthly*, Bulletin 22, 1955, pp. 1–4.

36. "From Bill Cody to Bill Faulkner," *Princeton University Library Chronicle*, XVII (Summer 1956), pp. 185–90.

37. "On Translating Faulkner," *Princeton University Library Chronicle,* XVIII (Spring 1957), pp. 108–13.

38. "L'art de la traduction," *Bulletin de la société des professeurs français en Amérique,* 1960, pp. 17–23.

In Spanish

39. "Erskine Caldwell," *La Nación,* 13 enero 1934.

40. "Actualidad del siglo XVI," *La Nación,* 1 abril 1934.

41. "Lluvia de estrellas," *La Nación,* 16 septiembre 1934.

42. "El realismo mágico," *La Nación,* 8 septiembre 1935.

43. "A propósito de la última novela publicada por William Faulkner," *La Nación,* 15 marzo 1936.

44. "Dos nuevas obras de Erskine Caldwell," *La Nación,* 15 marzo 1936.

45. "La tragedia de Ernest Hemingway," *La Nación,* 19 abril 1936.

46. "Thomas Wolfe, el aprendiz de brujo," *La Nación,* 18 octubre 1936.

47. "James T. Farrell y los irlandeses de Chicago," *La Nación,* 14 marzo 1937.

48. "Panorama de la actual literatura joven americana," *Sur,* marzo 1937, pp. 49–65.

49. "John Dos Passos, novelista, poeta y dramaturgo," *La Nación,* 2 mayo 1937.

50. "La sociedad francesa y la novela contemporánea," *La Nación,* 12 diciembre 1937.

51. "La guerra civil y la novela norteamericana," *La Nación,* 30 noviembre 1938.

52. "Acerca de algunos cuentos de John Steinbeck," *La Nación,* 23 abril 1939.

53. "John Steinbeck y la novela social," *La Nación,* 13 agosto 1939.

54. "A propósito de una novela póstuma de Thomas Wolfe," *La Nación,* 5 noviembre 1939.

55. "Norteamericanos de Montparnasse," *La Nación,* 14 enero 1940.

56. "El Premio Harper de literatura," *La Nación,* 4 febrero 1940.

57. "Los Campesinos vistos por William Faulkner," *La Nación,* 9 junio 1940.

58. "El Culto de la brutalidad en dos novelas recientes," *Sur,* LXXI (agosto 1940), pp. 62–65.

59. "Ernest Hemingway y la revolución española," *La Nación,* 8 diciembre 1940.

60. "Erskine Caldwell," *Sur,* LXXVI (enero 1941), pp. 77–100; LXXVII (febrero 1941), pp. 49–59.

61. "Acerca de la muerte de Scott Fitzgerald," *La Nación,* 9 marzo 1941.

62. "Libros de imágenes," *La Nación,* 1 febrero 1942.

63. "Están en boga las novelas de guerra," *La Nación,* 13 diciembre 1942.

64. "Muchachas y novelistas," *La Nación,* 9 enero 1944.

65. "Entrevista con Julien Green," *Sur,* CXXIII (enero 1945), pp. 49–61.

D. Book and Play Reviews:

1. "Louise Delpit: *Paris Theatre Counterpoint,*" *Modern Language Notes,* IV (April 1926), pp. 277–79.

2. "*Manhattan Transfer,*" *La Revue nouvelle,* XVIII (15 mai 1926), p. 614.

3. "Un nouveau livre de John Dos Passos: *Orient Express,*" *La Revue nouvelle,* XXXIII–XXXIV (septembre 1927), pp. 63–66.

4. "M. Sinclair Lewis mange du curé," *La Revue de siècle,* 15 décembre 1927, pp. 345–48.

5. "Une nouvelle comédie de George Kelly: *Philip Goes Forth,*" *La Revue nouvelle,* mars 1931, pp. 85–88.

6. "Luis Cons: *Anthologie littéraire de la Renaissance française,*" *Modern Language Notes,* X (June 1932), p. 416.

7. "John Dos Passos: *1919,*" *La Nouvelle revue française,* CCXXXVII (août 1932), pp. 313–16.

8. "Ernest Hemingway: *Death in the Afternoon,*" *La Nouvelle revue française,* CCXXXVII (novembre 1932), pp. 778–81.

9. "D. H. Lawrence en Amérique (Mabel Dodge Luhan: *Lorenzo en Taos*)," *Cahiers du sud,* mars 1933, pp. 216–19.

10. "*Le Paris:* Raman Fernandez; *Les Amours enfantines,* III, *Eros de Paris,* IV: Jules Romains (*Les Hommes de bonne volonté*)," *French Review,* VI (April 1933), pp. 421–22.

11. "*Sabine, Les Fiançailles:* Jacques de Lacretelle; *La Vie des Crapauds:* Jean Rostand," *French Review,* VI (May 1933), pp. 500–501.

12. "*Light in August,*" *La Nouvelle revue française,* CCXXXIX (1 août 1933), pp. 302–305.

13. "*Le Cheval blanc:* M. Hofer; *Les Pieds dans le plat:* René Crevel; *Été:* Marianne Commene," *French Review,* VII (December 1933), pp. 156–57.

14. "*Les Superbes,* V, *Les Humbles,* VI: Jules Romains (*Les Hommes de bonne volonté*); *Le Chef à l'étoile d'argent:* Jean Peyre," *French Review,* VII (April 1934), pp. 418–19.

15. "*Justine:* Roger Couderc; *Les Quatre femmes de Philippe II:* Marcel Dhanys," *French Review,* VII (May 1934), pp. 488–89.

16. "*Tobacco Road:* Erskine Caldwell; *From Flushing to Calvary:* E. Dahlberg," *La Nouvelle revue française,* CCL (1 juillet 1934), pp. 125–29.

17. "*La Autobiografía de Gertrude Stein,*" *Sur,* IX, año IV (julio 1934), pp. 171–75.

18. "*Les Vendéennes:* B. Gabory; *Les Endiablés:* Ernest Perochon," *French Review,* VIII (December 1934), pp. 155–56.

19. "*Más allá del bien y del mal, February Hill:* Virginia Lincoln," *La Nación,* 6 enero 1935.

20. "*Psychologie de la littérature américaine:* Ludwig Lewisohn," *La Nouvelle revue française,* CCLXIV (1 septembre 1935), pp. 436–41.

21. "*Recherche d'une église, Province:* Jules Romains (*Les Hommes de bonne volonté*)," *French Review,* IX (November 1935), pp. 61–63.

22. *"Naissance:* Marcelle Auclair," *French Review,* IX (December 1935), pp. 159–60.

23. *"God's Little Acre:* Erskine Caldwell," *La Nouvelle revue française,* novembre 1936.

24. *"Les Soirs de l'archipel:* Jacques Boulenger," *French Review,* X (December 1936), pp. 157–58.

25. *"Montée des Périls, Les Pouvoirs:* Jules Romains *(Les Hommes de bonne volonté),"* *French Review,* X (December 1936), pp. 159–60.

26. "William Faulkner y su último gran libro," *La Nación,* 13 diciembre 1936.

27. *"Absalom, Absalom!* William Faulkner," *La Nouvelle revue française,* CCLXXX (1 janvier 1937), pp. 123–26.

28. *"Tovaritch:* Jacques Deval, edited by Frederic Ernst and Helene Harvitt," *French Review,* X (January 1937), pp. 234–35.

29. *"Ménaces de Mort:* Robert Bourget-Pailleron," *French Review,* X (March 1937), pp. 419–20.

30. *"The Novel of Adolescence in France:* Justin O'Brien," *The Romanic Review,* XXVIII (December 1937), pp. 375–79.

31. "Ernest Hemingway vuelve a la novela," *La Nación,* 30 enero 1938.

32. *"To Have and Have Not,"* *La Nouvelle revue française,* CCXCIV (1 mars 1938), pp. 500–504.

33. *"Hommes et oeuvres du XXᵉ siècle:* Henri Peyre," *The Romanic Review,* XXX (October 1939), pp. 311–15.

34. *"Ronsard, Prince of Poets:* Morris Bishop," *The Romanic Review,* XXXII (February 1941), pp. 86–89.

35. *"Memories of Happy Days:* Julian Green," *The Chimera,* I, no. 3 (1943), pp. 45–48.

36. *"Requiem for a Nun,"* *France-Amérique,* 8 octobre 1951.

E. PREFACES AND INTRODUCTIONS:

(Coindreau wrote the preface for each volume in this category except those for which he is listed as author of the introduction.)

1. *Lumière d'août.* William Faulkner. 1935.

2. *Le Roman régionaliste américain.* Pierre Brodin. Paris: G.-F. Maisonneuve, 1937.

3. *Le Bruit et la fureur.* William Faulkner. 1938.

4. *Nous les vivants.* Erskine Caldwell. Traduit par Ed. Michel-Tyl. 1938.

5. *Des Souris et des hommes.* John Steinbeck. 1939. Préface: Joseph Kessel; Introduction: Maurice Edgar Coindreau.

6. *Morceaux choisis de Jules Romains.* New York: Editions de la Maison de France, 1941. Introduction: Maurice Edgar Coindreau.

7. *Un Pauvre Type.* Erskine Caldwell. 1945.

8. *La Feuille repliée.* William Maxwell. 1948.

9. *Les Domaines hantés.* Truman Capote. 1949.

10. *Les Palmiers sauvages.* William Faulkner. 1952.

11. *La Maison d'haleine.* William Goyen. 1954.

12. *Jeux de Mains.* Juan Goytisolo. 1956.

13. *Inventions et pérégrinations d'Alfanhui.* Rafael Sánchez Ferlosio. 1957.

14. *Sissi mon fils adoré.* Miguel Delibes. Traduit par J. Francis Reille. 1958.

15. *La Sagesse dans le sang.* Flannery O'Connor. 1959. Introduction: Maurice Edgar Coindreau.

16. *Le Masque.* Elena Quiroga. Avec Bernard Sesé. 1959.

17. *Chronique d'une île.* Juan Goytisolo. Traduit par Robert Marrast. 1961.

18. *L'Orée des bois.* Heather Ross Miller. Traduit par Michel Gresset. 1967

19. *La Rose blanche de Memphis.* Col. W. C. Falkner. Traduit par Madeleine Jambon. Julliard, 1970.

F. Miscellaneous:

1. *Trois pièces d'epouvante.* André de Lorde. New York: Henry Holt & Company, 1925.

2. *Actualité du XVIe siècle: Mélanges offerts à Paul Laumonier.* Paris: E. Droz, 1925.

3. *Eddy et Paddy.* Avec Abel Hermant. Introduction, notes, et vocabulaire. Boston: D. C. Heath & Company, 1936.

4. *An Alternative French Composition Book.* Avec L. F. H. Lowe. New York: Henry Holt & Company, 1936.

5. *Contes et nouvelles du temps présent.* Avec J. R. Loy. New York: Reynal & Hitchcock, 1941.

6. *La Farce est jouée.* New York: Editions de la Maison Française, 1942. Préface: Simone de Caillavet Maurois.

7. *Quadrille américain, I: Les oeuvres nouvelles.* New York: Editions de la Maison Française, 1942.

8. *Quadrille américain, II: Les oeuvres nouvelles,* tome V. New York: Editions de la Maison Française, 1945.

9. *Aperçus de littérature américaine.* Paris, 1946.

INDEX

Loti, Pierre, xi
Louis XIV, 6
Lucifer With a Book, 197
Lugné-Poë, 4
Lumière d'août, xviii, 10, 11, 77, 88,
   94, 97, 100

Macbeth, 42
McCarthy, Mary, 197, 198, 199
McCloud, David, 187, 188
McCullers, Carson, 104, 127, 133
Machine à lire les pensées, La, 186n
McLoughlin, William G., Jr., 147
McPherson, Aimee Semple, xx,
   143–53
Madame Bovary, 5
Mademoiselle, 125
Maggie, A Girl of the Streets, 172
Magny, Claude-Edmonde, xviii, 19,
   66, 83
Magoon, Carey, 189
Maison Tellier, La, 172
Mallarmé, Stéphane, 15, 129, 135
Malraux, André, xvii, 9, 10, 19, 32,
   34, 65, 69, 79, 80, 94
Manet, Edouard, xiv
Manhattan Transfer, xii, xiii, xvi,
   8, 19, 76, 177
Mann, Thomas, 21
Manzini, Gianna, 160–61
Marble, Faun, The, 25
March, Joseph Moncure, 119
"March of the Martyrs, The," 151
Maritimes, Les, 185
Marks, Percy, 183
Maupassant, Guy de, 117, 172n
Maurois, André, 11, 19, 175, 186n
Maxwell, William, xvi, xix, 138,
   157–67, 183, 184
Melville, Herman, 158
Men of Good Will, 18
Millay, Edna St. Vincent, 182
Millay, Kathleen, 182, 196
Miller, Heather Ross, xiii
"Miriam," 125
Mohrt, Michel, 99, 103
Molière, 5, 103n
Monsieur Rabosson, 175
Montaigne, xxiii, 38, 59, 191
Montherlant, Henry de, 17
Moody, Millie Hite, 178

Morand, Paul, 179
Mort de quelqu'un, 9
Mort tout neuf, Un, 81
Mosquitoes, 25, 38, 56
Moussorgsky, 5
*Mrs. Eddy: The Biography of a
   Virginal Mind,* 148
Muir, Edwin, 139
"My Side of the Matter," 125

Naked Martini, The, 200
*Narrative of Arthur Gordon Pym,
   The,* 129
Nausée, La, xiv
Nemirovsky, Irene, 12
Nerval, Gérard de, 135
"New Notes on Edgar Poe," 56
New Yorker, 161, 189
New York Herald Tribune, 88
Nichols, John, 195
Nietzsche, 200
Night and Silence, Who Is Here? 199
Night of the Hunter, The, 153–54
Night on Bald Mountain, 44
Niles, Blair, 88
1919, 76
Not to Eat, Not for Love, 177
Nous les vivants, 121
Nouvelle revue française (N.R.F.) ,
   xvii, 9, 65, 80, 93, 94
Nowhere With Music, 180
N.R.F. *See Nouvelle revue française*

O'Connor, Flannery, xiii, xvi, xx,
   141–56
Of Mice and Men, xiii, xvi, 19
Of Time and The River, 189n
O'Hara, John, 199
O. Henry (prize) , 125
Ohnet, Georges, 6
"Old Man," xix, 52–62
Old Man and the Sea, The, 72–73
One Man's Initiation, 8, 177
Other Voices, Other Rooms,
   123–31, 138
Otway, Howard, 153

Paix des profondeurs, La, 47n
Palmiers sauvages, Les, 77, 80
Papinian, 192
Party at Cranton, The, 198